CYBERCRIME AND ITS IMPLICATIONS

CYBERCRIME AND ITS IMPLICATIONS

CHARLES DOYLE
EDITOR

Nova Science Publishers, Inc.
New York

For permission to use material from this book please contact us:
Telephone 631-231-7269; Fax 631-231-8175
Web Site: http://www.novapublishers.com

LIBRARY OF CONGRESS CATALOGING-IN-PUBLICATION DATA

Doyle, Charles.
Cybercrime and its implications / Charles Doyle.
p. cm.
Includes bibliographical references and index.
ISBN 978-1-60692-254-5 (softcover)
1. Computer crimes--United States. 2. Computer networks--Law and legislation--United States--Criminal provisions. 3. Internet--Law and legislation--United States--Criminal provisions. 4. Data protection--Law and legislation--United States. I. Title. II. Title: Cyber crime and its implications.
KF9350.D695 2009
345.73'0268--dc22

2008047888ISBN: 978-1-60692-254-5

Published by Nova Science Publishers, Inc. ✢ New York

CONTENTS

PREFACE

The federal computer fraud and abuse statute, 18 U.S.C. 1030, outlaws conduct that victimizes computer systems. It is a computer security law. It protects federal computers, bank computers, and computers connected to the Internet. It shields them from trespassing, threats, damage, espionage, and from being corruptly used as instruments of fraud. It is not a comprehensive provision, but instead it fills crack and gaps in the protection afforded by other federal criminal laws. This is a brief sketch of section 1030 and some of its federal statutory companions.

Subsection 1030(b) makes it a crime to attempt to commit any of these offenses. Subsection 1030(c) catalogs the penalties for committing them, penalties that range from imprisonment for not more than a year for simple cyberspace trespassing to a maximum of life imprisonment when death results from intentional computer damage. Subsection 1030(d) preserves the investigative authority of the Secret Service. Subsection 1030(e) supplies common definitions. Subsection 1030(f) disclaims any application to otherwise permissible law enforcement activities. Subsection 1030(g) creates a civil cause of action of victims of these crimes.

Excerpted from CRS Report 97-1025, Cybercrime: An Overview of the Federal Computer Fraud and Abuse Statute and Related Federal Criminal Laws, dated February 25, 2008.

SUMMARY

The federal computer fraud and abuse statute, 18 U.S.C. 1030, outlaws conduct that victimizes computer systems. It is a computer security law. It protects federal computers, bank computers, and computers connected to the Internet. It shields them from trespassing, threats, damage, espionage, and from being corruptly used as instruments of fraud. It is not a comprehensive provision, but instead it fills crack and gaps in the protection afforded by other federal criminal laws. This is a brief sketch of section 1030 and some of its federal statutory companions.

In their present form, the seven paragraphs of subsection 1030(a) outlaw:

- computer trespassing (e.g., hacking) in a government computer, 18 U.S.C. 1030(a)(3);
- computer trespassing (e.g., hackers) resulting in exposure to certain governmental, credit, financial, or commercial information, 18 U.S.C. 1030(a)(2);
- damaging a government computer, a bank computer, or a computer used in interstate or foreign commerce (e.g., a worm, computer virus, Trojan horse, time bomb, a denial of service attack, and other forms of cyber attack, cyber crime, or cyber terrorism), 18 U.S.C. 1030(a)(5);
- committing fraud an integral part of which involves unauthorized access to a government computer, a bank computer, or a computer used in interstate or foreign commerce, 18 U.S.C. 1030(a)(4);
- threatening to damage a government computer, a bank computer, or a computer used in interstate or foreign commerce, 18 U.S.C. 1030(a) (7);
- trafficking in passwords for government, bank computer, or computer used in interstate or foreign commerce, 18 U.S.C. 1030(a)(6); and
- accessing a computer to commit espionage, 18 U.S.C. 1030(a)(1).

Subsection 1030(b) makes it a crime to attempt to commit any of these offenses. Subsection 1030(c) catalogs the penalties for committing them, penalties that range from imprisonment for not more than a year for simple cyberspace trespassing to a maximum of life imprisonment when death results from intentional computer damage. Subsection 1030(d) preserves the investigative authority of the Secret Service. Subsection 1030(e) supplies common definitions. Subsection 1030(f) disclaims any application to otherwise permissible law enforcement activities. Subsection 1030(g) creates a civil cause of action of victims of these crimes.

This report is available in abbreviated form – without the footnotes, citations, quotations, or appendices found in this report – under the title Cybercrime: A Sketch of 18 U.S. C. 1030 and Related Federal Criminal Laws, RS20830.

INTRODUCTION

The federal computer fraud and abuse statute, 18 U.S.C. 1030, [1] protects computers in which there is a federal interest – federal computers, bank computers, and computers used in interstate and foreign commerce. It shields them from trespassing, threats, damage, espionage, and from being corruptly used as instruments of fraud. It is not a comprehensive provision, instead it fills cracks and gaps in the protection afforded by other state and federal criminal laws. It is a work that over the last three decades, Congress has kneaded, reworked, recast, amended, and supplemented to bolster the uncertain coverage of the more general federal trespassing, threat, malicious mischief, fraud, and espionage statutes [2]. This is a brief description of section 1030 and its federal statutory companions. There are other laws that address the subject of crime and computers. Section 1030 deals with computers as victims; other laws deal with computers as arenas for crime or as repositories of the evidence of crime or from some other perspective. These other laws – laws relating to identity theft, obscenity, pornography, gambling, inter alia – are beyond the scope of this report [3].

In their present form, the seven paragraphs of subsection 1030(a) outlaw:

- computer trespassing in a government computer, 18 U.S.C. 1030(a)(3);
- computer trespassing resulting in exposure to certain governmental, credit, financial, or commercial information, 18 U.S.C. 1030(a)(2);
- damaging a government computer, a bank computer, or a computer used in interstate or foreign commerce, 18 U.S.C. 1030(a)(5);
- committing fraud an integral part of which involves unauthorized access to a government computer, a bank computer, or a computer used in interstate or foreign commerce, 18 U.S.C. 1030(a)(4);
- threatening to damage a government computer, a bank computer, or a computer used in interstate or foreign commerce, 18 U.S.C. 1030(a) (7);

- trafficking in passwords for a government computer, a bank computer, or a computer used in interstate or foreign commerce, 18 U.S.C. 1030(a)(6); and
- accessing a computer to commit espionage, 18 U.S.C. 1030(a)(1).

Subsection 1030(b) makes it a crime to attempt to commit any of these offenses [4]. Subsection 1030(c) catalogs the penalties for committing them, penalties that range from imprisonment for not more than a year for simple cyberspace trespassing to imprisonment for not more than twenty years for a second espionage- related conviction. Subsection 1030(d) preserves the investigative authority of the Secret Service. Subsection 1030(e) supplies common definitions. Subsection 1030(f) disclaims any application to otherwise permissible law enforcement activities. Subsection 1030(g) creates a civil cause of action for victims of these crimes. And subsection 1030(h) called for annual reports through 1999 from the Attorney General and Secretary of the Treasury on investigations under the damage paragraph (18 U.S.C. 1030(a)(5)).

Chapter 1

TRESPASSING IN GOVERNMENT CYBERSPACE (18 U.S.C. 1030(A) (3)))

Whoever . . . intentionally, without authorization to access any nonpublic computer [5] of a department or agency of the United States, [6] accesses such a computer of that department or agency that is exclusively for the use of the Government of the United States or, in the case of a computer not exclusively for such use, is used by or for the Government of the United States and such conduct affects that use by or for the Government of the United States . . . shall be punished as provided in subsection (c) of this section.

(b) Whoever attempts to commit an offense under subsection (a) of this section shall be punished as provided in subsection (c) of this section.

Paragraph 1030(a)(3) condemns unauthorized intrusion ("hacking") into federal government computers whether they are used exclusively by the government or the government shares access with others. With the help of subsection 1030(b) it also outlaws attempted intrusions. In the case of shared computers, a crime only occurs if the unauthorized access "affects . . . use by or for" the government or would affect such use if an attempted effort had succeeded.

Broken down into its elements, paragraph (a)(3) makes it unlawful for anyone to:

- without authorization
- intentionally
- either

access a government computer maintained exclusively for the use of the federal government, or access a government computer used, at least in part, by or for the federal government and the access affects use by or for the federal government, or attempt to do so (18 U.S.C. 1030(b)).

This pure trespassing proscription dates from 1986 and its legislative history leaves little doubt that nothing more than unauthorized entry is required:

> "[S]ection 2(b) will clarify the present 18 U.S.C. 1030(a)(3), making clear that it applies to acts of simple trespass against computers belonging to, or being used by or for, the Federal Government. The Department of Justice and others have expressed concerns about whether the present subsection covers acts of mere trespass, i.e., unauthorized access, or whether it requires a further showing that the information perused was 'used, modified, destroyed, or disclosed.' To alleviate those concerns, the Committee wants to make clear that the new subsection will be a simple trespass offense, applicable to persons without authorized access to Federal computers," S.Rept. 99-432 at 7 (1986); see also, H.Rept. 99-612 at 11 (1986).

Intent

The paragraph only bans "intentional" trespassing. The reports are instructive here, for they make it apparent that the element cannot be satisfied by a mere inadvertent trespass and nothing more. It is intended, however, to cover anyone who purposefully accomplishes the proscribed unauthorized entry into a government computer, and, at least in the view of the House report, anyone "whose initial access was inadvertent but who then deliberatively maintains access after a non-intentional initial contact," H.Rept. 99-612 at 9-10 (1986); see also, S.Rept. 99-432 at 5-6 (1986).

Unauthorized Access

While the question of what constitutes "access without authorization" might seem fairly straight forward, Congress was willing to accept a certain degree of trespassing by government employees in order to protect whistleblowers:

> The Committee wishes to be very precise about who may be prosecuted under the new subsection (a)(3). The Committee was concerned that a Federal computer crime statute not be so broad as to create a risk that government employees and others who are authorized to use a Federal Government computer

would not face prosecution for acts of computer access and use that, while technically wrong, should not rise to the level of criminal conduct. At the same time, the Committee was required to balance its concern for Federal employees and other authorized users against the legitimate need to protect Government computers against abuse by "outsiders." The Committee struck that balance in the following manner.

In the first place, the Committee has declined to criminalize acts in which the offending employee merely 'exceeds authorized access' to computers in his own department ("department"' is defined in section 2(g) of S.2281 [now 18 U.S.C. 1030(e)(7)]). It is not difficult to envision an employee or other individual who, while authorized to use a particular computer in one department, briefly exceeds his authorized access and peruses data belonging to the department that he is not supposed to look at. This is especially true where the department in question lacks a clear method of delineating which individuals are authorized to access certain of its data. The Committee believes that administrative sanctions are more appropriate than criminal punishment in such a case. The Committee wishes to avoid the danger that every time an employee exceeds his authorized access to his department's computers – no matter how slightly – he could be prosecuted under this subsection. That danger will be prevented by not including "exceeds authorized access" as part of this subsection's offense.

In the second place, the Committee has distinguished between acts of unauthorized access that occur within a department and those that involve trespasses into computers belonging to another department. The former are not covered by subsection (a)(3); the latter are. Again, it is not difficult to envision an individual who, while authorized to use certain computers in one department, is not authorized to use them all. The danger existed that S.228 1, as originally introduced, might cover every employee who happens to sit down, within his department, at a computer terminal which he is not officially authorized to use. These acts can also be best handled by administrative sanctions, rather than by criminal punishment. To that end, the Committee has constructed its amended version of (a)(3) to prevent prosecution of those who, while authorized to use some computers in their department, use others for which they lack the proper authorization. By precluding liability in purely 'insider' cases such as these, the Committee also seeks to alleviate concerns by Senators Mathias and Leahy that the existing statute cases a wide net over "whistleblowers". . . .

The Committee has thus limited 18 U.S.C. 1030(a)(3) to cases where the offender is completely outside the Government, and has no authority to access a computer of any agency or department of the United States, or where the offender's act of trespass is interdepartmental in nature. The Committee does not intend to preclude prosecution under this subsection if, for example, a Labor Department employee authorized to use Labor's computers accesses without authorization an FBI computer. An employee who uses his department's computer and, without authorization, forages into data belonging to another department is engaged in conduct directly analogous to an 'outsider' tampering with Government computers. . . .

The Committee acknowledges that in rare circumstances this may leave serious cases of intradepartmental trespass free from criminal prosecution under (a)(3). However, the Committee notes that such serious acts may be subject to other criminal penalties if, for example, they violate trade secrets laws or 18 U.S.C. 1030(a)(1), (a)(4), (a)(5), or (a)(6), as proposed in this legislation. S.Rept. 99-432 at 7-8 (1986); see also, H.Rept. 99-612 at 11 (1986).

Affects the Use

Trespassing upon governmental computer space on computers that are not exclusive for governmental use is prohibited only when it affects use by the government or use for governmental purposes. The committee reports provide a useful explanation of the distinctive, "affects-the-use" element of the trespassing ban:

> [T]respassing in a computer used only part-time by the Federal Government need not be shown to have affected the operation of the government as a whole. The Department of Justice has expressed concerns that the present subsection's language could be construed to require a showing that the offender's conduct would be an exceedingly difficult task for Federal prosecutors. Accordingly, Section 2(b) will make clear that the offender's conduct need only affect the use of the Government''s operation of the computer in question [or the operation of the computer in question on behalf of the Government]. S.Rept. 99-432 at 6-7 (1986); see also, H.Rept. 99-6 12 at 11 (1986); S.Rept. 104-357 at 9 (1996).

Jurisdiction

The reports offer little insight into the meaning of the third element – what computers are protected from trespassing. There may be two reasons. Paragraph 1030(a)(3) protects only government computers and therefore explanations of the sweep of its coverage in the area of interstate commerce or of financial institutions are unnecessary. Besides, at least for purposes of these trespassing offenses of paragraph 1030(a)(3), the statute itself addresses several of the potentially more nettlesome questions.

First, the construction of the statute itself strongly suggests that it reaches only computers owned or leased by the federal government: "whoever . . . without authorization to access any nonpublic computer of a department or agency of the United States, accesses such a computer of that department or agency. . . ."

Second, the language of the statute indicates that "nonpublic" computers may nevertheless include government computers that the government allows to be used by nongovernmental purposes: "in the case of a [government] computer not exclusively for the use of the Government of the United States . . . ."

Third, the statute covers government computers that are available to nongovernment users: "accesses such a computer . . . that . . . in the case of a [government] computer not exclusively for the use of the Government of the United States, is used by or for the Government of the United States . . . ." The use of the term "nonpublic," however, makes it clear that this shared access may not be so broad as to include the general public.

Finally, the section supplies a definition of "department of the United States": "[a] s used in this section . . . the term 'department of the United States' means the legislative or judicial branch of the Government or one of the executive departments enumerated in section 101 of title 5," 18 U.S.C. 1030(e) (7); [7] and the title supplies a definition of "agency of the United States": "[a]s used in this title . . . [t]he term 'agency' includes any department, independent establishment, commission, administration, authority, board or bureau of the United States or any corporation in which the United States has a proprietary interest, unless the context shows that such term was intended to be used in a more limited sense," 18 U.S.C. 6.

Extraterritorial Jurisdiction. There is one jurisdictional aspect of paragraph 1030(a)(3) that is unclear. Under what circumstances, if any, does the paragraph reach hacking initiated or occurring overseas? As a general rule, federal criminal laws are presumed to apply within the United States and not overseas. In some instances, Congress explicitly negates the presumption. The treason statute, for example, outlaws the offense whether committed "within the United States or elsewhere," 18 U.S.C. 2381.

In other instances, when the criminal statute is silent, the courts will conclude that Congress must have intended the statute to apply to overseas misconduct because of the nature of the offense and the circumstances under which it was committed. For example, the Supreme Court concluded that Congress must have intended the federal statute that prohibited fraud against the federal government to apply to fraud against the United States committed abroad, particularly when the offenders were Americans [8] The Court later decided that a federal statute that outlawed conspiracy to violate federal law applied to an overseas conspiracy to smuggle liquor into this country. [9]

In the cybercrime context, at least one court determined that paragraph 1030(a)(4), which prohibits unauthorized computer access to defraud, applied to a hacker in Russia who gained unauthorized access to "protected computers" in this country [10]. The court's conclusion was influenced by an amendment in which Congress had added computers used in "foreign commerce or communications" to the definition of "protected computers" and by the legislative history of why it did so [11]. While the case was pending, Congress further amended the definition of "protected computer" to include "a computer located outside the United States that is used in a manner that affects interstate or foreign commerce or communication of the United States," 18 U.S.C. 1030(e)(2)(B).[12]

Paragraph 1030(a)(3) does not cover "protected computers;" it covers nonpublic, federal government computers. Congress explicitly provided extraterritorial jurisdiction over the computer-related information acquisition, fraud, damage, and extortion offenses by amending the definition of protected computer. It provided no such explicit provision for simple trafficking offense under paragraph 1030(a)(3).

A court might conclude that Congress meant both to grant extraterritorial application in computer-related information acquisition, fraud, damage, and extortion cases under paragraphs 1030(a)(2), (4), (5), and (7) and to foreclose extraterritorial application in simple trespassing cases under paragraph 1030(a)(3) – even under circumstances when the courts would have otherwise found it appropriate in a simple trespassing case.

Penalties

The penalties for violation or attempted violation of paragraph 1030(a)(3) imprisonment for not more than one year and/or a fine of not more than $100,000 ($200,000 for organizations) for the first offense and imprisonment for not more than 10 years and/or a fine of not more than $250,000 ($500,000 for organizations) for all subsequent convictions, 18 U.S.C. 1030(c), 3571 [13].

Offenses under other paragraphs may trigger forfeiture, restitution, racketeering, money laundering, sentencing guidelines, and civil liability provisions elsewhere in the law. For reasons that will become apparent when they are discussed later in this report, those provisions have little, if any, relevance in case of simple trespassing offenses under paragraph 1030(a)(3).

Juveniles. Historically, federal authorities did not prosecute juvenile offenders. Most federal crimes, including computer hacking, are crimes under the laws of most states. When a juvenile violates a federal law, he must be turned over to state juvenile authorities unless the state is unwilling or unable to proceed against him, or unless the state has inadequate facilities for his treatment, or unless the crime is a violent federal felony or a federal drug or firearms offense, 18 U.S.C. 5032 [14].

Overview. Paragraph 1030(a)(3) has remained essentially unchanged since 1986, [15] and there appear to have been relatively few prosecutions under its provisions [16]. The explanation may be that paragraph 1030(a)(3) tracks paragraph 1030(a)(2) so closely that the prosecution is ordinarily reserved for the more serious cases which warrant the more serious felony sanctions available under information acquisition offense of paragraph 1030(a)(3), but not the simple trespassing offense of paragraph 1030(a)(2) [17].

Other Crimes [18]

Attempt. An attempt to hack into a federal computer in violation of paragraph 1030(a)(3) is also a federal crime, 18 U.S.C. 1030(b). In fact, subsection 1030(b) makes it a federal crime to attempt to violate any of the paragraphs of subsection 1030(a) [19]. The subsection dates from the original enactment and evokes no comment in the legislation history other than the notation of its existence, H.Rept. 98-894 at 22 (1984).

This is not particularly unusual. There is no general federal attempt statute, [20] but Congress has elected to penalize attempts to commit many individual federal crimes [21]. A body of case law has grown up around them that provides a common understanding of their general dimensions. Thus, as a general rule, in order to convict a defendant of attempt, the government must prove beyond a reasonable doubt that, acting with the intent required to commit the underlying offense, [22] the defendant took some substantial step towards the commission of the underlying offense [23] that strongly corroborates his criminal intent [24]. Mere preparation does not constitute a substantial step.25 The line between preparation and a substantial step towards final commission depends largely upon the facts of a particular case, [26] and the courts have offered varying descriptions of its location [27].

Conspiracy. Conspiracy to violate any federal law is a separate federal crime, 18 U.S.C. 371, [28] Thus, if two or more individuals agree to intentionally access a government computer without authorization and one of them takes some affirmative action to effectuate their plan, each of the individuals is guilty of conspiracy under section 371, regardless of whether the scheme is ultimately successful; [29] and if a conspirator manages to "hack" into a government computer, his coconspirators are equally guilty under 18 U.S.C. 1030(a)(3) [30].

Accomplices as Principals. By the same token, one who counsels, commands, aids or abets, or otherwise acts as an accessory before the fact is liable as a principal for the underlying substantive offense to the same extent as the individual who actually commits the offense [31]. More than mere inadvertent assistance is required; but an accomplice who embraces the criminal objectives of another and acts to bring about their accomplishment is criminally liable as a principal [32].

The fact that subsection 1030(b) outlaws attempts to violate any of the prohibitions of subsection 1030(a) raises an interesting question concerning accessories. As a general rule, an accomplice may only be liable as a principal or accessory before the fact, for a completed crime; the aid must be given before the crime is committed, but liability as a principal will not attach until after the crime has been committed [33]. This does not bar conviction of one who aids or abets the commission of a crime that never succeeds beyond the attempt phase, if, as in the case of paragraph 1030(a)(3), attempt to commit the offense has been made a separate crime [34].

CAN-SPAM & E-mail. Beyond these auxiliary offenses and bases for criminal liability, the simple trespassing crime created in paragraph 103 0(a)(3) is the least likely of the seven crimes established in section 1030 to share coverage with other laws outside the section. Simply hacking into government computers – without damage to the system, injury to the government, or gain by the hacker – implicates only a few other laws.

The most likely overlap may be with the CAN-SPAM Act of 2003, 18 U. S.C. 1037. The CAN-SPAM Act offers protection to all "protected computers" [35] and prohibits any unauthorized access of these computers for the purpose of sending commercial electronic messages (paragraph 1 037(a)(1)), or the purpose of deceiving or misleading e-mail recipients (paragraph 1037(a)(2)). The penalties involved for a violation of CAN-SPAM can be as high as five years imprisonment, if done in furtherance of a felony, or three years for a violation of paragraph 1037(a)(1) or if there is any financial loss by the victim or gain by the hacker, or one year "in any other case," 18 U.S.C. 1037(b) [36].

Of course computer trespassing in one form or another is an element of most of the offenses proscribed in 18 U.S.C. 1030. In addition, each of the states has an anti- hacking statute [37]. Moreover, hacking into someone else's e-mail stored in a government computer system is likely to offend the federal statute that protects email and stored telephone company records, 18 U.S.C. 2701 [38]. Hackers who misidentify themselves in order to gain access to a federal computer may be guilty of violating 18 U.S.C. 1001 [39] and 18 U.S.C. 912 [40] in the view of at least one commentator [41]. The case law may make the claim difficult to defend. The Supreme Court has suggested that section 1001 should be constructed narrowly, [42] and the courts have consistently held that the false statement must somehow tend to adversely impact the functioning of a governmental agency or department to trigger coverage under section 1001 [43] Cases in other contexts demonstrate the difficulty of convincing the courts that simple trespassing in government cyberspace has an adverse impact upon the government [44].

The difficulty with using the impersonation statute, 18 U.S.C. 912, is that it requires a showing of an official act or of a fraud; something that need not be proven for conviction under paragraph 1030(a)(3) [45]. Like 18 U.S.C. 1001, section 912 may be more appropriately employed in cases falling under the ambit of paragraph 1030(a)(4) (unauthorized access of a government computer, bank computer or computer in interstate or foreign commerce as integral part of a scheme to fraud).

Chapter 2

OBTAINING INFORMATION BY UNAUTHORIZED COMPUTER ACCESS (18 U.S.C. 1030(A)(2))

> *(a) Whoever . . . (2) intentionally accesses a computer without authorization or exceeds authorized access, and thereby obtains – information contained in a financial record of a financial institution, or of a card issuer as defined in section 1602(n) of title 15, [46] or contained in a file of a consumer reporting agency on a consumer, as such terms are defined in the Fair Credit Reporting Act (15 U.S. C. 1681 et seq.); [47] information from any department or agency of the United States; or (C) information from any protected computer if the conduct involved an interstate or foreign communication . . .shall be punished as provided in subsection (c) of this section.*

One step beyond simple hacking is the prohibition against acquiring certain protected information by intentional unauthorized access [48]. As a practical matter, in any instance involving a government computer it may be very difficult to distinguish between cases evidencing a violation of the simple trespass proscriptions of paragraph 1030(a)(3) and the trespassing-with-information-acquisition prohibitions of paragraph 1030(a)(2). The history of the trespass provisions speaks clearly of an intent to place beyond their reach whistleblowers and other federal employees for simple trespassing with respect to computers within their own an agency. This explains the absence of an "exceeds-authorized-access" provision in the trespassing provisions of paragraph 1030(a)(3). But the trespass-and-be-exposed-to-information provisions of paragraph 1030(a)(2) do feature a "exceeds-authorized-access" clause and seem facially applicable to whistleblowers. It remains to be seen whether the courts will read paragraph 1030(a)(2) as effectively amending the simple trespassing provisions of paragraph 1030(a)(3) or will attempt to reconcile the two.

Intent

The intent requirement is the same as that required in the case of simple trespassing. The offender must have "intentionally" gained access. The paragraph only bans "intentional" trespassing. As in the case of the simple trespassing the intent element can be satisfied by anyone who purposefully gains access to a computer covered by the paragraph or by anyone "whose initial access was inadvertent but who then deliberatively maintain access after a non-intentional initial contact." [49]. The government, however, need not show that the trespass was committed to defraud or for any other purpose for that matter [50].

Unauthorized Access

"Without authorization" or "exceeds authorized access" under 1030(a)(2) has been construed to apply to access by authorized current employees who use their access in any unauthorized manner or for unauthorized purposes, to former employees, and to outsiders who have been granted access subject to explicit reservations [51]. Access within the statute, however, does not mean simply passively receiving information from a computer [52].

Obtaining Information and Jurisdiction

Paragraph 1030(a)(2) is at once more and less restricted than the simple trespassing proscription of paragraph 1030(a)(3). On one hand, its prosecution requires more than simple trespass [53]. On the other hand, it covers a wider range of computers. Paragraph 1030(a)(2), unlike 1030(a)(3), covers more than government computers. It covers computers from which three types of information may be obtained – information of the federal government, consumer credit or other kinds of financial information, and information acquired from a protected computer through interstate or foreign access.

The protection for financial information has its origins in the initial legislation and was among the first adjusted. Comments from the Senate report accompanying the 1986 amendments illustrate the intended scope of the protection for financial information:

> "The premise of 18 U.S.C. 1030(a)(2) will remain the protection, for privacy reasons, of computerized credit records and computerized information relating to

customers' relationships with financial institutions. This protection is imperative in light of the sensitive and personal financial information contained in such computer files. However, by referring to the Right to Financial Privacy Act, the current statute limits its coverage to financial institution customers who are individuals, or are partnerships with five or fewer partners. The Committee intends . . . to extend the same privacy protections to the financial records of all customers – individual, partnership, or corporate – of financial institutions.

"The Department of Justice has expressed concerns that the term 'obtains information' in 18 U.S.C. 1030(a)(2) makes that subsection more than an unauthorized access offense, i.e., that it might require the prosecution to prove asportation of the data in question. Because the premise of this subsection is privacy protection, the Committee wishes to make clear that 'obtaining information' in this context includes mere observation of the data. Actual asportation, in the sense of physically removing the data from its original location or transcribing the data, need not be proved in order to establish a violation of this subsection," S.Rept. 99-432 at 6-7 (1986).

The committee explanation of the language amending paragraph 1030(a)(2), ultimately enacted as part of the Economic Espionage Act of 1996, endorsed this reading and extended it to cover information obtained from federal computers and information secured by interstate or overseas cyberspace trespassing:

"'Information' as used in this subsection [1030(a)(2)] includes information stored in intangible form. Moreover, the term 'obtaining information' includes merely reading it. There is no requirement that the information be copied or transported. This is critically important because, in an electronic environment, information can be 'stolen' without asportation, and the original usually remains intact. This interpretation of 'obtaining information' is consistent with congressional intent expressed . . . in connection with 1986 amendments to the Computer Fraud and Abuse statute . . . .

"The proposed subsection 1030(a)(2)(C) is intended to protect against the interstate or foreign theft of information by computer. This information, stored electronically, is intangible, and it has been held that the theft of such information cannot be charged under more traditional criminal statutes such as Interstate Transportation of Stolen Property Act, 18 U.S.C. 2314. See United States v. Brown, 925 F.2d 1301, 1308 (10th Cir. 1991). This subsection would ensure that the theft of intangible information by the unauthorized use of a computer is prohibited in the same way theft of physical items are protected. In instances where the information stolen is also copyrighted, the theft may implicate certain rights under the copyright laws. The crux of the offense under subsection 1030(a)(2)(C), however, is the abuse of a computer to obtain the information," S.Rept. 104-357 at 6-7 (1996).

The Patriot Act amendment of the definition of "protected computer" confirmed Congress' intent to proscribe unauthorized access and information acquisition from abroad with respect to protected computers [54]. A closer question may be whether in doing so it forecloses extraterritorial application of paragraph 1030(a)(2) in other situations, e.g., unauthorized access to federal computer or computer networks located overseas.

Consequences

The simple trespass offenses condemned in paragraph 1030(a)(3) are unlikely to significantly implicate the Sentencing Guidelines, restitution, forfeiture, or civil liability provisions elsewhere in the law. Not so paragraph 1030(a)(2) offenses. Criminal penalties attend it, but so do other consequences.

Penalties. Paragraph 1030(a)(2) has a three tier sentencing structure. Simple violations are punished as misdemeanors, imprisonment for not more than one year and/or a fine of not more than $100,000 ($200,000 for organizations), 18 U.S.C. 1030(c)(2)(A).

The second tier carries penalties of imprisonment for not more than five years and/or a fine of not more $250,000 ($500,000 for organizations) and is reserved for cases in which: "(i) the offense was committed for purposes of commercial advantage or private financial gain; (ii) the offense was committed in furtherance of any criminal or tortious act in violation of the Constitution or laws of the United States or of any State; or (iii) the value of the information obtained exceeds $5,000," 18 U.S.C. 1030(c)(2) (B).

This second level was added in 1996. The $5,000 threshold is the same one the section uses to separate serious from less serious fraud and destruction cases in paragraphs 1030(a)(4) and 1030(a)(5). With respect to the alternative thresholds, (i) and (ii), "[t]he terms 'for purposes of commercial advantage or private financial gain' and 'for the purpose of committing any criminal or tortious act' are taken from the copyright statute (17 U.S.C. 506(a)) and the wiretap statute (18 U.S.C. 2511[(2)] (d)), respectively, and are intended to have the same meaning as in those statutes," S.Rept. 104-357 at 8 (1996). The references to copyright and wiretap law may be less instructive than Congress anticipated for the phrases in question are of uncertain meaning in their original settings.55 Nevertheless, they clearly contemplate some criminal, tortious, or financially advantageous purpose beyond the computertrespassing-and-obtaining-information misconduct outlawed in the paragraph generally. Otherwise nothing would be left to be punished as a misdemeanor and the $5,000 distinction of exception (iii) would be swallowed up as well.

The third tier is for repeat offenders whose punishment is increased to imprisonment of not than 10 years and/or a fine of not more than $250,000 ($500,000 or organizations) for a second or subsequent conviction, 18 U.S.C. 1030(c).

Federal law is no more hospitable to the prosecution of juveniles for the intrusion plus information acquisition offenses under paragraph 1030(a)(2) than it is for the simple trespass offenses under paragraph 1030(a)(3). Essentially, federal proceedings are only possible if the state in which the offense occurs is unwilling or unable to proceed, 18 U.S.C. 5032.

Sentencing Guidelines. The Sentencing Guidelines color the procedure under which the penalties for serious federal crimes are imposed [56]. They were established to eliminate sentencing disparity among cases involving the same offense and to ensure that the sentences imposed reflect the relative seriousness of the circumstances under which the offense was committed in a given case [57] As a general rule, the Guidelines assign each federal crime to a particular guideline [58]. The individual guideline in turn assigns a beginning number (base offense level) and then adds and subtracts from that number based on the presence of designated aggravating or mitigating circumstances [59]. The final total translates to an authorized sentencing range in months of imprisonment and dollars of fines [60].

Violations of paragraph 1030(a)(2) are governed by U.S. S.G. §2B 1.1 which sets the base offense level at 6. The Tenth Circuit's opinion in Willis provides an example of the process from that point:

> The District Court agreed with the Government and found Ms. Fischer's conduct [which resulted in losses of more than $10,000] foreseeable to [her accomplice] Mr. Willis. It therefore imposed a 4-level enhancement on Mr. Willis's base offense level [61].
>
> It also applied the §2B 1.1 (b)(1 0)(C)(i) enhancement because the offense involved using a means of identification to produce another means of identification, [62] as well as the §3B1.3 enhancement because Mr. Willis abused a position of trust [63]. This produced an adjusted offense level of 14, which when coupled with his criminal history category of V, resulted in an advisory Guideline range of 33 to 41 months. The District Court sentenced Mr. Willis to 41 months' imprisonment [64].

Forfeiture. "Any property, real or personal, which constitutes or is derived from proceeds traceable, to a violation of section . . . 1030" is subject to confiscation by the United States under either civil or criminal forfeiture procedures [65].

Restitution. Restitution is an offender's compensation of the victim for loss or damage associated with the offense [66]. It is mandatory in the case of federal crimes of violence or federal crimes involving fraud or property damage, 18 U.S.C. 3 663A [67]. It is within the discretion of the court in the case of all other federal crimes proscribed in title 18 of the United States Code, 18 U.S.C. 3663.

Paragraph 1030(a)(2) acquisition offenses are not crimes of violence and restitution is therefore not mandatory. They come within the discretionary restitution provisions of section 3663, but those provisions have a limitation on the type of losses for which restitution may be ordered [68]. The limitation, however, does not apply in the case of a plea bargain [69] or when restitution is orders as a condition of probation or supervised release [70].

Civil Cause of Action. Subsection 1030(g) creates a cause of action for compensatory damages and injunctive relief for the benefit of victims of a violation of any the paragraphs of 18 U.S.C. 1030, but only if violation results in the kind of loss or damage described in clauses 1030(a)(5)(B)(i) through (v), [71] that is:

> (i) loss to 1 or more persons during any 1-year period (and, for purposes of an investigation, prosecution, or other proceeding brought by the United States only, loss resulting from a related course of conduct affecting 1 or more other protected computers) aggregating at least $5,000 in value;
> (ii) the modification or impairment, or potential modification or impairment, of the medical examination, diagnosis, treatment, or care of 1 or more individuals;
> (iii) physical injury to any person;
> (iv) a threat to public health or safety; or
> (v) damage affecting a computer system used by or for a government entity in furtherance of the administration of justice, national defense, or national security [72].

There is no need to prove that a violation of paragraph 1030(a)(5) has occurred. As long as this type of loss or damage has been suffered, a violation of any of the paragraphs will suffice, including a violation of paragraph 1030(a)(2) [73].

At one time there may have been some uncertainty over the range of victims and losses envisioned in subsection 1030(g). Victims entitled to relief are described as "any person who suffers loss or damage by reason of a violation of this section," but until recently there was no specific definition of the term "person" in either section 1030 or in the definitions applicable to Title 18 generally [74]. The legislative history offered no further edification and the courts had not addressed the issue. "Person" can mean individuals, or individuals and other legal entities including governmental entities, or individuals and other legal entities but not including governmental entities [75] Credible arguments might have been made for each of the possible definitions, but the fact that Congress elected to use the term "person" to mean only individuals in paragraph 1030(a)(7)(extortionate threats) [76] might seem to favor those who call for a similar interpretation of subsection 1030(g). The USA PATRIOT Act resolved the issue by supplying a definition: "the term 'person' means any individual, firm, corporation, educational institution, governmental entity, or legal or other entity," 18 U.S.C. 1030(e)(12).

It also added a generous definition of the kinds of losses that might give rise to civil liability – "the term 'loss' means any reasonable cost to any victim, including the cost of responding to an offense, conducting a damage assessment, and restoring the data, program, system, or information to its condition prior to the offense, and any revenue lost, cost incurred, or other consequential damages incurred because of interruption of service," 18 U.S.C. 1030(e)(1 1). The amendment has obvious benefits for the victims of a paragraph (a)(2) intrusion and information acquisition offense with post-intrusion investigation and system evaluation costs but who otherwise would be unable to meet the $5,000 loss requirement of clause 1030 (a)(5)(B)(i)

Subsection 1030(g) suits must be brought within two years of the offense, and compensatory damages are limited to economic damages, 18 U.S.C. 1030(g).

Other Crimes

Attempt, Conspiracy, and Complicity. The same general observations concerning attempt, conspiracy and aiding and abetting noted for the simple trespass offense apply here. It is a separate crime to attempt to violate paragraph 1030(a)(2) under 18 U.S.C. 1030(b). Those who attempt to violate its provisions or aid and abet the violation of another are subject to the same penalties as those who commit the substantive offense, 18 U.S.C. 1030(c)(2). Conspirators to violate paragraph 1030(a)(2) are subject to the same penalties as the underlying offense, and to liability for any foreseeable crime committed in furtherance of the scheme [77].

Paragraph 1030(a)(2) is somewhat unique. There are a host of other federal conversion statutes, but all of the others appear to require that the offender either commit embezzlement by failing to comply with some fiduciary obligation or commit larceny by intending to acquire the property or to deprive another of it. Paragraph 1030(a)(2) in contrast to the conversion statutes and to the computer fraud provisions of paragraph 1030(a)(4) requires no larcenous intent [78]. As a practical matter, it essentially gives prosecutors a more serious charge against hackers, who do more than simply breach the outskirts of a governmental system, than would be available under the pure trespassing provisions of paragraph 1030(a)(3). And it gives them an alternative or additional charge, along with conversion and fraud statutes, against hackers who "steal" information from a protected computer [79]. It affords victims similar latitude in civil litigation under subsection 1030(g).

Paragraph 1030(a)(2) is essentially paragraph 1030(a)(3) plus an information acquisition element and with a broader jurisdictional base. Criminal prohibitions like those of 18 U.S.C. 1001 (false statements on a matter with the jurisdiction of a federal agency) or 912 (impersonating a federal official) which overlap with paragraph 1030(a)(3) at the point of unauthorized entry will overlap with paragraph 1030(a)(2) at the same point. If unauthorized access in violation of paragraph 1030(a)(3) is acquired by false statement under facts sufficient supporting a prosecution under 18 U.S.C. 1001 (false statements) or 18 U.S.C. 912 (false impersonation), unauthorized access and the acquisition of information in violation of paragraph 1030(a)(2) acquired by false statement or impersonation is likely to subject offender to prosecution under sections 1001 or 912 as well. By the same token, if unauthorized computer access to a voice mail or e-mail communication that violates paragraph 1030(a)(3) offends 18 U.S.C. 2511 (interception of wire or electronic communications) and 2701 (unauthorized acquisition of communications in electronic storage), unauthorized computer access and acquisition of information in violation of paragraph 1030(a)(2) is likely to violate sections 2511 and 2701 [80].

In fact, overlap is even more likely. Paragraph 1030(a)(3) protects only federal computers. Paragraph 1030(a)(2) protects not only federal computer information, but information from "protected computers" (computers used in interstate and foreign commerce) when the unauthorized access involves an interstate or foreign communication. Due to the nature of Internet communications, a communication may involve interstate communications even if the both the parties are located within the same state; [81] and, by virtue of an amendment in the USA PATRIOT Act, protected computer information may include information on computers located overseas as long as they involve or affect the foreign commerce or communications of the United States [82].

Interstate or Foreign Transportation of Stolen Property. Whether a hacker, who steals information stored in a computer, violates any of the general federal theft statutes depends upon whether the particular statute covers intangible property, and if not, whether the victim has been defrauded of tangible in addition to intangible property. For instance, the Supreme Court has noted that 18 U. S.C. 2314, that outlaws the interstate transportation of stolen goods, wares, or merchandise, [83]

> "contemplate[s] a physical identity between the items unlawfully obtained and those eventually transported." [84] Thus, the theft of information stored in a computer may be prosecuted under section 2314 only if the government can establish that it was accomplished in conjunction with the theft and transportation of a physical item. Downloading information onto a stolen computer disk and then transporting the disk across a state line is covered, yet downloading information onto a computer disk that is transported but not stolen is not covered; however, courts have begun to differ in this interpretation and some have found an electronic file to be a tangible good within the meaning of section 2314 [85].

The federal statute proscribing theft from interstate carriers, 18 U.S.C. 659, speaks in terms of stealing "goods and chattels" under a variety of circumstances [86]. And it is presumably subject to the same analysis: section 659 applies only to the theft of physical items; even if all of the other elements are satisfied, computer fraud is proscribed by section 659 only where in involves the theft of physical item.

Theft of Federal Government Information. Prosecuting computer fraud under a statute that outlaws the interstate transportation of stolen "goods, wares, merchandise, securities or money" may be an awkward fit. The general theft of government property statute, 18 U.S.C. 641, seems a better match, however, for that provision outlaws the misappropriation of any "thing of value" belonging to or in the possession of the federal government [87]. The courts have applied section 641 to the misappropriation of property that lacks any necessary corporal features [88].

Economic Espionage. Paragraph 1030(a)(2) overlaps with the Economic Espionage Act when the information acquired through unauthorized access is a trade secret [89]. The Economic Espionage Act, among other things, outlaws computerized burglary committed in a commercial setting, 18 U.S.C. 1 832 [90]. It makes it a federal crime to steal certain trade secrets, or to receive such trade secrets with the knowledge they have been stolen, or to conspire or attempt to steal them, or to conspire or attempt to receive them knowing they have been stolen. To be covered by the protective umbrella of section 1832, information must (1) have a nexus interstate or foreign commerce; (2) be a secret; and (3) have some trade value.

Information meets the commerce nexus when it is associated with a product that is marketed across state lines, i.e., if it is "related to or included in a product that is produced for or placed in interstate or foreign commerce," 18 U.S.C. 1832(a). Information is considered "secret" if it is "not generally known to the public or to the business, scientific, or education community in which [its] owner might seek to use the information" and its owner takes reasonable steps to maintain its confidentiality, H.Rept. 788 at 12; 18 U.S.C. 1839(3).

But what makes section 1832 a particularly effective shield against computerized burglary in a commercial setting is that the trade secret information it protects includes "all forms and types of financial, business, scientific, technical, economic, or engineering information, including patterns, plans, compilations, program devices, formulas, designs, prototypes, methods, techniques, processes, procedures, programs, or codes, whether tangible or intangible, and whether or how stored, compiled, or memorialized physically, electronically, graphically, photographically, or in writing," 18 U.S.C. 1839(3).

Violations of section 1832 are punishable by imprisonment for not more than 10 years and/or a fine of not more than the greater of twice the amount of pecuniary gain or loss resulting from the offense or $250,000 (not more than $5 million if the offender is an organization).

Copyright infringement. Downloading information after unauthorized access to a protected computer may violate not only paragraph 1030(a)(2) but may constitute copyright infringement as well. Computer software programs are ordinarily protected by copyright which generally precludes copying of protected material without the consent of the holder of the copyright. Copyright law outlaws three forms of willful copyright infringement: (A) infringement for "commercial advantage or private financial gain," 17 U.S.C. 506(a)(1)(A); (B) infringement by reproduction of distribution of protected works worth more than $1,000, 17 U.S.C. 506(a)(1)(B); and (C) infringement by "distribution of a work being prepared for commercial distribution, by making it available on a computer network accessible to members of the public, if such person knew or should have known that the work was intended for commercial distribution," 17 U.S.C. 506(a)(1)(C).

Each of the three forms of infringement has its own penalty structure under 18 U.S.C. 2319. Infringement for profit or commercial advantage is punishable by imprison terms with maximum limits of 1 to 10 years depending on the extent of the violation.91 The maximum term of imprisonment for infringement on works worth more than $1,000 ranges from 1 to 6 years [92]. Finally, the infringement involving works in preparation for distribution carries maximum penalties ranging from 3 to 10 years [93]. The offenses are also subject to fines of not more than $250,000 (not more than $500,000 for organizations) if the maximum term of imprisonment is more than 1 year, and otherwise of not more than $100,000 (not more than $200,000 for organizations) [94].

Money Laundering. The principal federal money làundering statutes, 18 U.S.C. 1956 and 1957, outlaw various financial activities that involve the proceeds from other federal crimes [95] They prohibit:

- domestic laundering of the proceeds of these predicate offenses, referred to as "specified unlawful activities;"
- international laundering of the proceeds of predicate offenses;
- using the proceeds of predicate offenses to promote further predicate offenses; [96] or
- spending or depositing more than $10,000 of the proceeds of predicate offenses [97]

Offenses under the various paragraphs of 18 U.S.C. 1030 are all money laundering predicate offenses, [98] although paragraph 1030(a)(2) information acquisition offenses are less likely to generate proceeds than are the fraud and espionage offenses of paragraphs 1030(a)(4) and 1030(a)(1).

Chapter 3

CAUSING COMPUTER DAMAGE (18 U.S.C. 1030(A)(5))

Whoever . . . (5)(A)(i) knowingly causes the transmission of a program, information, code, or command, and as a result of such conduct, intentionally causes damage [99] without authorization, to a protected computer;[100]

(ii) intentionally accesses a protected computer without authorization, and as a result of such conduct, recklessly causes damage; or

(iii) intentionally accesses a protected computer without authorization, and as a result of such conduct, causes damage; and

(B) by conduct described in clause (i), (ii), or (iii) of subparagraph (A), caused (or, in the case of an attempted offense, would, if completed, have caused) –(i) loss to 1 or more persons during any 1-year period (and, for purposes of an investigation, prosecution, or other proceeding brought by the United States only, loss resulting from a related course of conduct affecting 1 or more other protected computers) aggregating at least $5,000 in value;

(ii) the modification or impairment, or potential modification or impairment of medical examination, diagnosis, treatment, or care of 1 or more individuals;

(iii) physical injury to any person;

(iv) a threat to public health or safety; or

(v) damage affecting a computer system used by or for a government entity in furtherance of the administration of justice, national defense, or national security . . . shall be punished as provided in subsection (c) of this section.

Intent

Paragraph 1030(a)(5) establishes crimes of dual intent – the intent to knowingly intrude and the intent to damage. Hackers or the creators of viruses, worms and the like may trigger paragraph 1030(a)(5), when they damage, even unintentionally, the systems they have knowingly invaded [101]. Paragraph 1030(a)(5) establishes three computer damage offenses, distinguishable on the basis of the offender's intent to cause damage: (1) causing damage to a protected computer by intentional unauthorized access; (2) recklessly causing damage to a protected computer by intentional unauthorized access; and (3) intentionally causing damage to a protected computer through a knowing transmission. This feature, added in 1996 and amended in the USA PATRIOT and Homeland Security Acts, punishes recklessly and intentionally caused damage more seriously but preserves the earlier understanding that anyone who intentionally secures unauthorized access is punishable for any resulting damage regardless of whether they intended to cause it, or were recklessly indifferent as to whether they did so [102]. In simple terms, to establish a violation a defendant must shown to have "(1) intentionally accessed (2) a protected computer (3) without authorization, and (4) as a result of such conduct, has (5) intentionally, recklessly, or otherwise caused (6) damage." [103]

Unauthorized Activity

Unauthorized activity under paragraph 1030(a)(5) takes two forms. For the intentional damage offense of clause 1030(a)(5)(A)(i), the offender must knowingly transmit a command, program, information or code thereby intentionally causing unauthorized damage. For the reckless or simple damage offenses of clauses 1030(a)(5)(A)(ii) and (iii), the offender must intentionally access a computer without authorization and thereby cause damage either recklessly or unintentionally. In the first instance, it is the damage that is unauthorized; in the second and third it is the access to the computer. The Justice Department suggests that one reason for the distinction is that damage can be intentionally caused without having to access the victimized computer directly, [104] so that the clause reaches intentional damage whether through direct access or not [105]. The legislative history seems to confirm this view [106]. Of course, the clause applies to direct access as well. It reach any individual who intentionally causes damage by issuing a destructive command or downloading a destructive program, after having accessed the victimized computer whether with authorization, without authorization, or in excess of authorization. While the other clauses refer to unauthorized access and exceeding authorized access, clause (a)(5)(a)(i) speaks of unauthorized damage. There is some precedent for the view that "unauthorized damage" includes by implication damage in excess of authorization [107].

To establish the transmission element of the intentional damage offense, "the government must offer sufficient proof that the person charged is the same person who sent the transmission. Circumstantial evidence is sufficient to prove that the transmission occurred." [108]

As for unauthorized access element of clauses (a)(5)(A)(ii) and (iii), when the other paragraphs of 18 U.S.C. 1030 speak of unauthorized access, they mention "exceeding authorized access" as an alternative [109]. Clauses (a)(5)(A)(ii) and (iii) do not; they speak only of unauthorized access. The difference has been construed to mean that only outsiders may violation the reckless and simple damage clauses [110].

Damage

Not all computer damage qualifies as the damage element of a paragraph 1030(a)(5) offense. The paragraph extends to only five specific kinds of damage inflicted upon a specific class of computers. The damage must be an "impairment to the integrity or availability of data, a program, a system, or information," [111] that:

- causes a loss over the course a year exceeds $5,000; [112]
- modifies, impairs, or could modify or impair medical services;
- causes physical injury;
- threatens public health or safety; or
- affects a justice, national defense, or national security entity computer, 18 U. S.C. 1030(a)(5)(B).

The elements were added in 1996 without a great deal of individual commentary, [113] but the 1996 legislative history of related segments of the statute is informative. An earlier prohibition spoke of intrusions that "cause[d] loss or damage to one or more other persons of value aggregating $1,000 or more during any 1-year period," 18 U.S.C. 1030(a)(5)(A)(ii)(II)(1994 ed.)(emphasis added). The Senate Committee report observes that use of the term "damage" contemplates the inclusion of all economic harm attributable to the intrusion and that the increased dollar limitation is expected to restrict federal felony prosecutions to the more serious cases:

> "The 1994 amendment required both 'damage' and 'loss,' but it is not always clear what constitutes 'damage.' For example, intruders often alter

existing log-on programs so that user passwords are copied to a file which the hackers can retrieve later. After retrieving the newly created password file, the intruder restores the altered log-on file to its original condition. Arguably, in such a situation, neither the computer nor its information is damaged. Nonetheless, this conduct allows the intruder to accumulate valid user passwords to the system, requires all system users to change their passwords, and requires the system administrator to devote resources to resecuring the system. Thus, although there is arguably no 'damage,' the victim does suffer 'loss.' If the loss to the victim meets the required monetary threshold, the conduct should be criminal, and the victim should be entitled to relief. The bill therefore defines 'damage' in new subsection 1030(e)(8), with a focus on the harm that the law seeks to prevent. As in the past, the term 'damage' will require . . . significant financial losses," S.Rept. 104-357 at 11 (1996).

Ordinarily, the presence of a separate hacker prohibition with less severe penalties would argue against allowing "damage assessment" and "security enhancement" costs to be used to reach the $5,000 threshold for the more severe penalty. The report language might be read to rebut such a presumption, but it might also be characterized as asserting no more than that the cost of new locks ("resecuring the system") can be considered damage when the keys ("passwords") are stolen.

The USA PATRIOT Act reduced the prospect of misconception by supplying an explicit definition of "loss" as used here; "the term 'loss' means any reasonable cost to any victim, including the cost of responding to an offense, conducting a damage assessment, and restoring the data, program, system, or information to its condition prior to the offense, and any revenue lost, cost incurred, or other consequential damages incurred because of interruption of service," 18 U.S.C. 1030(e)(1 1). Thus, the losses incurred by a contractor employed to manage the damaged computer system may properly be included to reach the $5,000 threshold [114].

It also eliminated a second potential problem. The 1996 amendments, perhaps inadvertently, rephrased the aggregate $5,000 damage-loss threshold describing the victims as "individuals" rather than the term previously employed, "persons." [115]. The change stimulated contentions that Congress intended to limit the cases where the threshold could be reached entirely to the damages and losses suffered by human beings without any reference to the damages and losses suffered by corporate or other legal entities [116] The USA PATRIOT Act negated the problem by describing the damage-loss victims as "persons" and by defining persons to include individuals and any "legal or other entity," 18 U.S.C. 1030(a)(5)(B)(i), (e)(12).

The long standing medical tampering element has no monetary threshold and has remained essentially unchanged since it was added in response to an incident in which juvenile hackers broke into the computer system of the Sloan-Kettering Cancer Center [117].

The inclusion of computer tampering that causes physical injuries or threatens public health or safety, on the other hand, is new with the 1996 amendments and is designed to reach more general threats:

> As the NII [National Information Infrastructure] and other network infrastructures continue to grown, computers will increasingly be used for access to critical services such a emergency response systems and air traffic control, and will be critical to other systems which we cannot yet anticipate. S.Rept. 104-357 at 11 (1996).

Jurisdiction

These kinds of damage are only federal crimes under paragraph 1030(a)(5) if they involve a protected computer. There are five types of protected computers or computer systems. The five include computers:

- used exclusively for or by the United States government;
- used exclusively for or by a bank or other financial institution;
- used in part for or by the United States government where the damage "affects" the government use or use of the government's behalf;
- used in part for or by a bank or other financial institution where the damage "affects" use by or on behalf of the institution; and
- used in interstate or foreign commerce or communications including a computer outside the country whose use affects U.S. commerce, 18 U.S.C. 1030(e)(2).

What is a "computer . . . used in interstate or foreign commerce or communications"? The legislative history shows that the phrase means computer damage which might affect interstate or foreign commerce or interstate or foreign communications. The phrase appears in section 1030 after the 1994 amendments when it was first used to supplement (and in the 1996 amendments to replace) the phrase "computer . . . which is one of two or more computers used in committing the offense, not all of which are located in the same State," compare 18 U.S.C. 1030(a)(5), (e)(2)(1986 Supp.), with 18 U.S.C. 1030(a)(5), (e)(2)(1994 ed.). The change was made because under the earlier language "hackers who attacked other computers in their own State were not subject to Federal jurisdiction, notwithstanding the fact that their actions may have severely affected interstate or foreign commerce. For example, individuals who attack[ed] telephone switches m[ight] disrupt interstate and foreign calls. The 1994 change remedied that defect," S.Rept. 104-357 at 10 (1996). The inherently interstate nature of the Internet is such that a computer used to access the Internet is a computer used in interstate or foreign commerce, and consequently a computer whose protection is within Congress' power to regulate [118]

Precisely which government computers are protected is a bit more uncertain. Although terms used elsewhere in section 1030 such as "governmental entity" [119] and "department of the United States," are expressly defined, there is no definition of either the phrase "United States Government" or the phrase "Government of the United States" used from the beginning to described the scope of protection provided federal computers. The reports do not explain its meaning. In the trespassing provisions of paragraph 1030 (a)(3), however, the phrase is used in juxtaposition with the phrase "department or agency of the United States" [120] suggesting that the term embodies the meaning assigned to that phrase by the definitions subsection of section 1030 [121] and by the definition section generally applicable to title 18 of the United States Code [122]. On the other hand, it would not be unreasonable for a court to conclude that the phases "United States Government" and "Government of the United States" should be construed narrowly since when Congress intended an expansive definition it provided one. The definition of financial institutions whose computers are protected [123] differs only slightly from the definition generally applicable in title 18 [124].

The question persists as to whether by specifically mentioning overseas computers in the interstate and foreign commerce basis for jurisdiction ("including a computer outside the country whose use affects U.S. commerce"), Congress intended to preclude overseas application of the other bases for jurisdiction (e.g., damage to government computers).

Consequences

Penalties. The paragraph punishes causing damage recklessly or intentionally more severely than causing damage without necessarily intending to do. Causing damage, without necessarily intending to do so, by intentionally gaining access, or attempting to gain access, to a protected computer is punishable by imprisonment of not more than one year (not more than 10 years for a second or subsequent offense) and/or a fine of not more than $100,000 ($200,000 for organizations)(not more than $250,000/$500,0,00 for a second or subsequent offense) 18 U.S.C. 1030(c)(2)(A), (c)(3)(B); 18 U.S.C. 3571 [125].

Recklessly causing damage by intentionally gaining access, or attempting to gain access, to a protected computer is punishable by imprisonment for not more than five years (not more than 20 years for a second or subsequent offense) and/or a fine of not more than $250,000 (not more than $500,000 for an organization), 18 U.S.C. 1030(c)(4)(B); 18 U.S.C. 3571.

Intentionally causing damage through a knowing transmission to a protected computer is punishable by imprisonment for not more than 10 years (not more than 20 years for a second or subsequent offense) and/or a fine of not more than $250,000 (not more than $500,000 for an organization), 18 U.S.C. 1030(c)(4)(A); 18 U.S.C. 3571. An offender who knowingly or recklessly causes or attempts to cause serious bodily injury or death by knowingly causing an intentionally damaging transmission to a protected computer is punishable by imprisonment for not more than of 20 years (any term of years or life if death results) and/or fine of $250,000 ($500,000 for an organization), 18 U.S.C. 1030(c)(5), 18 U.S.C. 3571 [126].

Here as elsewhere, offenses committed by juveniles are more likely to result in state rather than federal proceedings [127]. Many of the other auxiliary provisions of law such as those relating to the Sentencing Guidelines, forfeiture, and the like, which have little relevance in the case of simple trespassing, may have real consequences in the case of the damage offenses proscribed in paragraph 18 U.S.C. 1030(a)(5).

Sentencing Guidelines. The Sentencing Guidelines operate in paragraph 1030(a)(5) damage cases much as they do in paragraph 1030(a)(2) information acquisition cases [128]. The offenses are assigned to the same guideline, U.S.S.G. §2B1.1. Some of that guideline's escalators, however, are more obviously relevant in damage cases. For example, there is a minimum enhancement of 4 levels when a paragraph 1030(a)(5) offense involves the intentional infliction of damage, [129] and another range of enhancements when an offense has multiple victims [130]. In addition, although the two offenses trigger the same range of enhancements based on the extent of loss or damage caused by the offense, the amount of damage or loss is often greater in a damage case [131].

Forfeiture and Restitution. Property derived from a violation of any paragraph of 18 U. S.C. 1030 is subject to confiscation [132]. Restitution is mandatory when related to a violation of a paragraph which proscribes fraud or property damage [133]. Forfeiture is judged largely by the extent of the offender's ill-gotten gains; restitution by the extent of the injuries caused by his offense. Thus, restitution is more commonly found in paragraph 1030(a)(5) damages cases than is forfeiture [134].

Cause of Action. Regardless of the criminal sanctions imposed, offenders of paragraph 1030(a)(2) may also incur civil liability for damage caused, 18 U.S.C. 1030(g) [135].

Victims of a violation of paragraph 1030(a)(5) or any violation of subsection 1030(a) resulting in the requisite harm have a cause of action for compensatory damages and equitable relief if suit is brought within two years [136]. Damages to medical records, or damage causing physical injury or endangering public safety may also subject the offender to "compensatory" damages beyond "economic" damages – a difference that may entitle a victim to pecuniary damages as well as damages for pain and suffering but probably not exemplary damages [137]. Damages caused by a simply knowing violation of paragraph 1030(a)(5) (as opposed to reckless and intentional violations) are limited to economic damages.

Victims are described as "any person who suffers loss or damage by reason of a violation of this section," but until recently there was no specific definition of the term "person" in either section 1030 or in the definitions applicable to Title 18 generally [138]. The legislative history offered no further edification and the provision has yet to be construed by the courts. "Person" could mean individuals, or individuals and other legal entities including governmental entities, or individuals and other legal entities but not including governmental entities. Creditable arguments can be made for each of the possible definitions, but the fact that Congress elected to use the term "person" to mean only individuals in paragraph 1030(a)(7)(extortionate threats) [139] might seem to favor a similar interpretation in subsection 1030(g). The USA PATRIOT Act resolved the question and answered several others.

First, it supplied a definition of person – "the term 'person' means any individual, firm, corporation, educational institution, governmental entity, or legal or other entity," 18 U.S.C. 1030(e)(12). Then, it added an equally generous definition of the kinds of losses that might give raise to civil liability – "the term 'loss' means any reasonable cost to any victim, including the cost of responding to an offense, conducting a damage assessment, and restoring the data, program, system, or information to its condition prior to the offense, and any revenue lost, cost incurred, or other consequential damages incurred because of interruption of service," 18 U.S.C. 1030(e)(1 1). Finally, it made clear that subsection 1030(g) does not create a cause of action for loss or damage attributable to "the negligent design or manufacture of computer hardware, computer software, or firmware," 18 U. S.C. 1030(g) [140].

Crimes of Terrorism. Paragraph (1) espionage offenses and paragraph (5) intentional damage offenses (other than those based on cause $5,000 in damage) are the only crimes under 18 U.S.C. 1030 classified as federal crimes of terrorism.141 Designation as a federal crime of terrorism triggers the application of several other substantive and procedural criminal statutes, without any further nexus to terrorism. Federal crimes of terrorism are subject to an 8-year statute of limitations rather than the 5-year period that governs most federal crimes [142]. The maximum term of supervised release for a federal crime of terrorism is life, rather than the 5-year maximum that applies in most other instances [143]. An individual charged with a federal crime of terrorism is presumed to be an inappropriate subject for release on bail prior to his criminal trial, 18 U.S.C. 3143(e). The maximum term of imprisonment for aggravated identity theft is 5 years when the offense is committed in relation to a federal crime of terrorism rather than the 2-year maximum that would otherwise apply, 18 U.S.C. 1028A. It is a separate federal crime punishable by imprisonment for any term of years or for life to knowingly provide maritime transportation to an individual intending to commit, or in flight from the commission of, a federal crime of terrorism, 18 U.S.C. 2284.

Federal crimes of terrorism are also by definition RICO predicate offenses, 18 U.S.C. 1961(1). Among other things, RICO outlaws the patterned commission of predicate offenses ("racketeering activities") in order to acquire or conduct the affairs of an enterprise whose activities affect interstate or foreign commerce [144]. Offenders face imprisonment for up to 20 years, 18 U.S.C. 1963, as well as civil liability.

Other Crimes

Attempt, Conspiracy, and Complicity

The same general observations concerning attempt, conspiracy and aiding and abetting noted for the simple trespass paragraph apply here. It is a separate crime to attempt to violate paragraph 1030(a)(5) or any of the other paragraphs of subsection 1030(a), 18 U.S.C. 1030(b). Those who attempt to violate or who aid and abet the violation of another are subject to the same penalties as those commit the substantive offense, 18 U.S.C. 1030(c), 2. The same is true of conspiracies except that conspiracy to commit a felony carries a five year maximum of imprisonment, 18 U.S.C. 371.

Damage or Destruction of Federal Property

There are more than a few other federal statutes that might be implicated by damage or destruction of federal property, of the property of financial institutions, or of property used in interstate or foreign commerce. The principal uncertainty is whether these general statutes can be applied to protect intangible property, like information in computer storage. Even if computer-stored data is considered tangible property (electronic files rather than paper files), several statutes that outlaw damage or destruction may be unavailable because they either call for a specific means of destruction – destruction by fire or explosives – or because they protect a particular kind of property – timber or buildings [145].

Destruction of Government Records. It is a federal crime for anyone to unlawfully "conceal, remove, mutilate, obliterate, or destroy . . . any record, proceeding, map, book, paper, document, or other thing, filed or deposited with . . . any judicial or public officer of the United States." [146]. The damage or destruction of government, computer-stored records will fall within the coverage of Section 2071 only if it can meet each of the action (obliterate or destroy), object (any record or other thing) and place (filled with a federal judicial or public officer) tests.

The phrase "conceal, remove, mutilate, obliterate, or destroy" may lend itself to the argument that it extends to destruction or complete inaccessibility, but perhaps not to less than totally destructive damage, of computerized records. Electronic destruction seems to fit under either "obliterate" ("to make undecipherable by obscuring") [147] or "destroy." Absent obliteration or destruction, the section may be thought to protect only tangibles, since the word "mutilate" has obvious physical connotations. Yet one court among the few to construe section 2071 held that it did not prohibit photocopying of government records – not because that would constitute the removal of an intangible (information), but because the statute was designed to prevent "any conduct which deprives the Government of the use of its documents." [148]

The phrase "any record, proceeding, map, book, paper, document, or other thing, filed or deposited with" would seem to cover any "thing" capable of being "filed or deposited". In these days of "electronic filing" [149] any contention that federal computer records do not fit the phrase seems untenable.

The final requirement might appear to protect only those records based on deposits with federal court or administrative officials, but the scant case law available suggests coverage extends to any record maintained by the government [150].

Violations of section 2071 are punishable by imprisonment for not more than three years and/or a fine of not more than $250,000, or both fine and imprisonment, 18 U.S.C. 2071, 3571.

Destruction of Federal Property. It is a federal crime to "willfully injure or commit any depredation against any property of the United States. . . ." [151] Although an offender must be shown to have to injure or depredate property, the government need not show that the defendant knew the property belonged to the government [152]. The federal courts have permitted prosecution under section 1361 of a defendant who used a hammer and drill to destroy a federal computer [153]. There are no reported cases in which section 1361 was used to prosecute electronic computer abuse for damaging federal property, and federal authorities used an earlier version of the computer abuse statute, section 1030, to prosecute one of the first cases of electronic computer abuse resulting in damage [154].

Damage or destruction of federal property is punishable by imprisonment for not more than 10 years and/or a fine of not more than $250,000 (or not more than one year and/or a fine of not more than $100,000 if the damage causes amounts to $1,000 or less and no one dies as a result of the offense), 18 U.S.C. 1361; 18 U.S.C. 3571.

Destruction of Federal Communications Systems. Willful or malicious interference or disruption "in any way" with any communications system owned by the United States or used by the United States for military or civil defense purposes is punishable by imprisonment for not more than 10 years and/or a fine of not more than $250,000 [155]. The language of section 1362 leaves little room for any contention that it does not apply to computer abuse aimed at federal communications facilities.

Damage or Destruction of Financial Institution Property

A handful of federal statutes protect financial institutions from theft in one form or another, but not property damage or destruction. Section 1030 appears to be the only statute that includes a specific provision designed to protect the property of financial institutions from damage or destruction. As with Morris, a defendant prosecuted under an earlier version of paragraph 1030(a)(5) questioned what level of intent was required with respect to the damage caused [156].

Damage or Destruction to Property in Interstate Commerce

Transportation. The federal statutes, other than paragraph 1030(a)(5), most likely to cover the computerized damage or destruction to property in interstate commerce involve transportation. Each of the provisions that proscribe interference with air, motor, rail and sea transportation appear to have been drafted with sufficient breadth to reach damage or destruction of at least some of the computer systems incidental to those transportation facilities.

For example, the provisions applicable to the destruction of aircraft and aircraft facilities penalize anyone who "damages, destroys, or disables any air navigation facility . . . if such . . . damaging, destroying, [or] disabling . . . is likely to endanger the safety of any such aircraft," 18 U. S.C. 32(a)(3) [157]. This would presumably protect air traffic control systems, but not computerized passenger information, i.e., gridlock is not proscribed unless it "endanger[s] the safety" of air travel.

The language of the provisions outlawing interference with maritime navigation are strikingly comparable: "a person who unlawfully and intentionally . . . destroys or seriously damages maritime navigational facilities or serious interferes with their operation, is such act is like to endanger the safe navigation of a ship" or attempts or conspires to do so is punishable by imprisonment for not more than 20 years and/or a fine of not more than $250,000, or if death results form commission of the offense, by imprisonment for life or death [158]. Federal jurisdiction for prosecution exists if the offense occurs within American territorial waters, if the vessel or vessels engaged are of American registry, or if committed by American or by someone later found in this country, 18 U.S.C. 2280(b).

Similarly, attacks on mass transit are punishable by imprisonment for not more than 20 years and/or a fine of not more than $250,000, if death results from commission of the offense, by imprisonment for life or death [159]. Once again, computer abuse that targets rail traffic control is almost certainly covered; computer abuse that targets ticket control is almost certainly not.

The language of the federal law outlawing the destruction of motor vehicle facilities seems only slightly more modest, for it extends to anyone who "with a reckless disregard for the safety of human life," willfully "damages, destroys . . . tampers with," or otherwise makes "unworkable, unusable, or hazardous to work or use" any "facility used in the operation of, or in support of the operation of, motor vehicles engaged in interstate or foreign commerce," 18 U.S.C. 33(a) [160]. Computer abuse that damages or destroys motor traffic control systems in a manner threatening to human safety would seem to fall within the reach of section 33.

Other Damage Crimes. Other federal crimes that might be implicated by damaging computer systems used in interstate or foreign commerce include those that cover damage to an energy facility [161] or proscribe interference with the operation of a communications or weather satellite [162]. Most of the states also outlaw damaging computer equipment, software, or systems [163].

RICO. Those paragraph 1030(a)(5) damage offenses that qualify as federal crimes of terrorism – damaging a protected computer and thereby impairing medical care, causing physical injury, or threatening public health or safety; or damaging a governmental justice, national defense, or national security computer system – are by virtue of that fact RICO predicate offenses [164]. Among other things, RICO outlaws conducting the business of a commercial enterprise through the patterned commission of predicate offenses [165].

Violations are punishable by (a) forfeiture of any property acquired through a RICO violation and of any property interest in the enterprise involved in the violation, and (b) imprisonment for not more than 20 years, or life if one of the predicate offenses carries such a penalty, and/or a fine of not more than $250,000, 18 U.S.C. 1963.

RICO violations also subject the offender to civil liability. The courts may award anyone injured by a RICO violation treble damages, costs and attorneys' fees, and may enjoin RICO violations, order divestiture, dissolution or reorganization, or restrict an offender's future professional or investment activities, 18 U.S.C. 1964.

Chapter 4

COMPUTER FRAUD (18 U.S.C. 1030(A)(4))

> *(a) Whoever . . . (4) knowingly and with intent to defraud, accesses a protected computer without authorization, or exceeds authorized access, and by means of such conduct furthers the intended fraud and obtains anything of value, unless the object of the fraud and the thing obtained consists only of the use of the computer and the value of such use is not more than $5,000 in any 1-year period . . . shall be punished as provided in subsection (c) of this section.*

Paragraph 1030(a)(4) outlaws fraud by computer intrusion. Its elements consist of:

- knowingly and with intent to defraud;
- accessing a protected computer without authorization, or exceeding authorization;
- thereby furthering a fraud and obtaining anything of value (other than a minimal amount of computer time, i.e., more than $5,000 over the course of a year) [166]

Jurisdiction

Paragraph 1030(a)(4) outlaws fraud against "protected computers," i.e., computers used in interstate or foreign commerce, 18 U.S.C. 1030(e)(2)(B), those used by or for "the United States Government," or those used by or for a financial institution, 18 U.S.C. 1030(e)(2)(A). As noted earlier, there may be some real doubt whether in doing so it reaches computers of the legislative and judicial branches or of the independent federal agencies, or whether it shields only those within the executive branch. The wording of some of the paragraphs of section

1030 clearly anticipates expansive coverage. Having declined to take advantage of those terms of art with respect to paragraph 1030(a)(4), should Congress be presumed to have intended a more limited reach? As noted earlier, the counterpoint is that in one paragraph of section 1030, Congress uses the phrase "Government of the United States" interchangeably with the more expansive phrase "department or agency of the United States," 18 U.S.C. 1030(a)(3). If the terms are interchangeable at one point within the section should they not be construed as interchangeable through out?

The Committee reports indicate that Congress understood the phrase "used in interstate or foreign commerce" to be the equivalent of "affecting interstate or foreign commerce," S.Rept. 104-357 at 10 (1996).

Congress amended the definition of protected computer used in interstate or foreign commerce by adding the phrase "including a computer located outside the United State that is used in a manner that affects interstate or foreign commerce," 18 U.S.C. 1030(e)(2). In doing so, it might be thought to have intended to preclude overseas application of the paragraphs of 18 U.S.C. 1030 under any other circumstances, e.g., a federal computer located outside the United States that is not used in a manner that affects commerce.

Intent

Paragraph 1030(a)(4) was proposed as part of the original statute in 1984, H.Rept. 98-894 at 27 (1984), but only enacted with the 1986 amendments, P.L. 99- 474, 100 Stat. 1213 (1986), 18 U.S.C. 1030 (1986 Supp.). The reports accompanying the 1986 amendments note that the intent element – "knowingly and with intent to defraud" – "is the same standard used for 18 U.S.C. 1029 relating to credit card fraud," S.Rept. 99-432 at 10 (1986); H.Rept. 99-612 at 12 (1986). The phrase as used in the credit card fraud statute means that the offender is conscious of the natural consequences of his action (i.e. that it is likely that someone will be defrauded) and intends that those consequences should occur (i.e., he intends that someone should be defrauded) [167].

The phrase "thereby furthers a fraud" insures that prosecutions are limited to cases where use of a computer is central to a criminal scheme rather those where a computer is used simply as a record-keeping convenience [168].

Similarly, the demand that the value of converted property exceed $5,000 avoids the possibility that mere computer trespassing would be prosecuted as fraud under the theory that lost computer time could satisfy the "thing of value" element that separates the two offenses. The $5,000 threshold overcomes this problem while permitting prosecution for repeated intrusions, S.Rept. 104-357 at 9 (1996).

The case law available thus far confirms that the difficulty of maintaining a prosecution against even a repeated trespasser under paragraph 1030(a)(4). As United States v. Czubinski, 106 F.3d 1069 (1st Cir. 1997), demonstrates. Czubinski involved an Internal Revenue Service employee who conducted a number of unauthorized searches of taxpayer files in an IRS computer system. The Court of Appeals overturned his conviction on four counts of violating paragraph 1030(a)(4) because it felt the government had failed to prove that the government had been defrauded, i.e, deprived of anything of value [169].

Consequences

Violations are punishable by imprisonment for not more than five years (not more than 10 years for subsequent offenses) and/or a fine of not more than $250,000 (not more than $500,000 for organizations), 18 U.S.C. 1030(c)(4); 18 U.S.C. 3571.170 The same sentencing guideline, U.S. S.G. §2B 1.1, covers both fraud under paragraph 1030(a)(4), and damage under paragraph 1030(a)(5), although the escalators based on the amount of loss inflicted are likely to be more telling in the case of wide-spread damage caused by the release of a worm or virus. As discussed earlier, conviction of a paragraph 1030(a)(4) offense requires an order to make restitution and may lead to the confiscation of the fruits of the offense, 18 U.S.C. 981(a)(1)(C), 982(a)(2)(B), 3663A. Victims may sue for compensatory damages and/or injunctive relief under subsection 1030(g) [171]

Other Crimes

Paragraph 1030(a)(4) prohibits unauthorized use of a government computer, a bank computer or a computer used in interstate or foreign commerce as an integral part of a fraud. Its companions at federal criminal law include general criminal statutes, statutes proscribing theft or fraud of federal property, those that outlaw the theft or fraud of the property of financial institutions, and those that prohibit theft or fraud involving property with an interstate or foreign commerce nexus.

Interstate and Foreign Commerce

Wire Fraud. Although the wire fraud statute, 18 U.S.C. 1343, does not refer to "things of value," a phrase that encompass both the tangible and the intangible, neither does it refer exclusively to physical items such as "goods, wares, merchandises, securities or money." Rather it condemns the use of interstate or foreign wire communications pursuant to a scheme to defraud another of "money or property." [172], The Supreme Court has made it clear that "property" within its purview may include confidential information, [173] and various federal courts have made it clear that confidential information in computer storage is no less favored [174]. In fact, one commentator claims that "[t]he wire fraud statute, 18 U.S.C. 1343, has produced more convictions for computer-related crimes than § 1030 or any other computer- specific statute." [175]

Credit Card Fraud. Section 1029 of title 18 (credit card fraud) and section 1030 (computer fraud) share a common recent history [176]. Like section 1030, section 1029 has undergone rather regular fine-tuning since its initial passage in 1984 as part of the Comprehensive Crime Control Act of that year [177]. Unlike section 1030, it has a single, uniformly applicable jurisdictional base: it applies to offenses that "affect interstate or foreign commerce." [178]

The two overlap where Section 1029 outlaws the deception of commercial computer systems through the improper use of an "access device" to acquire cash, credit, merchandise, or services [179]

An access device is

(1) any –

- card,
- personal identification number,
- plate,
- electronic serial number,
- code,
- mobile identification number, or
- any account number or other telecommunications service, equipment, or instrument identifier, or other means of account access;

(2) that either

a) can be used, alone or in conjunction with another access device, to obtain money, goods, services, or any other thing of value, or
b) can be used to initiate a transfer of funds (other than a transfer originated solely by paper instrument), 18 U.S.C. 1 029(e)(1).

The level of intent for each of the several crimes established in section 1029 is the same as that often used for section 1030 – "knowing and with the intent to defraud." Thus, criminal liability under section 1029 requires that the offender know that his or her actions are likely to deprive another of something of value and demands that the offender means for that deprivation to occur [180].

Section 1029 establishes three types of crimes: misuse of access devices, conduct in anticipation of misuse of access devices, and attempts or conspiracies to commit one of these substantive violations. The misuse crimes include:

- use of a counterfeit access device; [181] a counterfeit access device is one that is "counterfeit, fictitious, altered, or forged, or an identifiable component of an access device or a counterfeit access device" (§1 029(e)(2)(emphasis added)); [182]
- use of a unauthorized access device resulting in a loss or gain over the course of one year worth than $1,000; [183] an unauthorized access device is one that has been "lost, stolen, expired, revoked, canceled, or obtained with intent to defraud" (§1 029(e)(3)(emphasis added)); and
- use of an access device "issued to another person" resulting in a loss or gain over the course of one year worth than $1,000; again each of the uses is only criminal if done knowingly and with an intent to defraud; [184]

The "preparation" offenses of section 1029 each extend only to misconduct that affects interstate or foreign commerce and only to misconduct committed knowingly and with an intent to defraud, 18 U.S.C. 1029(a). They include:

- possession of 15 or more counterfeit or unauthorized access devices; [185]
- possession of "device-making" equipment (§1029(a)(4); [186] essentially counterfeiting paraphernalia; [187]
- offering another an access device or offering to sell information concerning an access device, without the authorization of the issue of the device; [188]
- use of a telecommunications device modified or altered to permit the unauthorized receipt of telecommunications services; [189]
- use of a scanner; [190] i.e., illegal wiretapping or electronic eavesdropping equipment; [191]
- possession of computer equipment used to avoid telecommunications charges, i.e., possession of "hardware or software used for altering or

modifying telecommunications instruments to obtain unauthorized access to telecommunications services"; [192] and

- causing another to present credit card slips for payment with the intent to defraud [193].

Paragraph 1029(b)(1) makes it a separate offense to attempt to commit any of the substantive crimes in subsection 1029(a) just described [194]. Paragraph 1 029(b)(2) makes it a separate offense to conspire to commit any of them [195]. Attempt to carries the same penalties as the completed offense (imprisonment either for not more than 10 or not more than 15 years), but conspiracy is punishable by imprisonment for not more than half the maximum terms applicable to the underlying offense (imprisonment for not more than 5 or not more than 7.5 years), 18 U.S.C. 1029(b). One reason for the distinction may be that while attempt is merged in the completed offense so that an offender may be punished for either but not both, the crime of conspiracy is ordinarily not merged in the substantive offense so that punishment for either or both is permitted.

In any event, the maximum penalties are determined by those set for the underlying violations of subsection 1029: (1) imprisonment for not more than 10 years for first time offenses involving:

- use of counterfeit access devices, 18 U.S.C. 1029(a)(1);
- use of unauthorized access devices, 18 U.S.C. 1029(a)(2);
- possession of 15 or more counterfeit or unauthorized access devices, 18 U.S.C. 1029(a)(3);
- unauthorized sale of an access device, 18 U.S.C. 1029(a)(6);
- possession of a device designed to avoid telephone charges, 18 U.S.C. 1029(a)(7); or
- fraudulently causing another to present credit car slips for payment, 18 U.S.C. 1029(a)(10);

and imprisonment for not more than 15 years for first time offenses involving:

- possession of counterfeiting equipment, 18 U.S.C. 1029(a)(4);
- use of another's access device to defraud, 18 U.S.C. 1029(a)(5);
- possession of a scanner, 18 U.S.C. 1029(a)(8); or
- possession of equipment designed to avoid communications service charges, 18 U.S.C. 1029(a)(9) [196].

Defrauding the Federal Government

Conspiracy. The same statute that makes it a crime to conspire to violate federal law also makes it a federal crime to conspire to defraud the United States, 18 U.S.C. 371 [197]. Unlike the mail and wire fraud statutes, a successful prosecution for conspiracy to defraud the United States does not require a showing that the defendant sought to deprive the United States or anyone else of money or property [198] This lesser known branch of the statute has extraordinary range and "reaches any conspiracy for the purpose of impairing, obstructing or defeating the lawful function of any department of the Government." [199] There need be no evidence of any other underlying substantive offense or purpose [200]. "The government need only show (1) that the defendant entered into an agreement (2) to obstruct a lawful function of the government (3) by deceitful or dishonest means and (4) at least one overt act in furtherance of the conspiracy." [201]

Fraud Involving Government Computers. There are also a host of federal criminal statutes that proscribe fraud in one form or other, more than a few of which would cover the unauthorized manipulation of federal computers as an integral part of a scheme to defraud. Two of the more prominent, the false statement statute, 18 U.S.C. 1001 (false statements on a matter within the jurisdiction of a federal agency or department) and conspiracy to defraud the United States, 18 U.S.C. 371, have already been mentioned. Others include 18 U.S.C. 1031 (major procurement fraud against the United States); [202] 18 U.S.C. 1035 (false statements relating to health care); [203] 18 U.S.C. 1014 (false statements on federally insured loan and credit applications); [204] 18 U.S.C. 1010, 1012 (false statements concerning various HUD transactions); [205] and 18 U.S.C. 287 (false claims against the United States) [206].

Bank Fraud. Although less numerous, several federal criminal statutes outlaw defrauding financial institutions in language similar to the prohibitions against defrauding the United States, most notably the general bank fraud provision, 18 U.S.C. 1344 [207] and the laws that proscribe embezzlement and similar misconduct by bank officers and employees [208].

General Crimes

CA N-SPA M Act. The criminal provisions of the Controlling the Assault of Non-Solicited Pornography and Marketing Act of 2003 (CAN-SPAM), 18 U.S.C. 1037, generally broadens the type of coverage given by section 1030 and adds to the federal government's ability to prosecute hackers who use e-mail for fraudulent purposes. More precisely, it proscribes, when done knowingly and in a manner in or affecting interstate or foreign commerce:

- accessing a protected computer and intentionally sending multiple e-mails (100 a day month, 1,000 a month, or 10,000 a year), 18 U.S.C. 1037(a)(1), (d)(3);
- using a protected computer to send commercial e-mails with the intent to deceive or mislead as to their source, 18 U.S.C. 1037(a)(2);
- materially altering an e-mail header and sending out multiple e-mails under the falsified header, 18 U.S.C. 1037(a)(3), (d)(3);
- registering for 5 or more e-mail accounts or 2 or domain names providing false identification and using them to send out multiple commercial e-mails, 18 U.S.C. 1037(a)(4), (d)(3); or
- providing false identification to registrant of 5 or more IP addresses and using the addresses to send out multiple commercial e-mails, or conspires to do so, 18 U.S.C. 1037(a)(5), (d)(3).

Offenders face one of a number of sentences ranging from imprisonment for not more than a year to imprisonment for not more than 5 years depending on the extent and regularity of the offense, among other factors [209]. When the offense is punishable by imprisonment for not more than a year, offenders also face to a fine of not more than $100,000 (not more than $200,000 for organizations); those guilty of other violations of section 1037 face fines of not more than $250,000 (not more than $500,000 for organizations), 18 U.S.C. 3571. Any property used in, or realized through, the commission of the offense is subject to confiscation, 18 U.S.C. 1037(c).

Attempt, Conspiracy, and Complicity. The same general observations concerning attempt, conspiracy and aiding and abetting noted for the simple trespass paragraph apply here. It is a separate crime to attempt to violate paragraph 1030(a)(4), 18 U.S.C. 1030(b). Those who attempt to do so or who aid and abet the violation of another are subject to the same penalties as those commit the substantive offense, 18 U.S.C. 1030(c), 2. The same is true of conspiracies except that conspiracy to commit a felony carries a five year maximum of imprisonment, 18 U.S.C. 371.

Money Laundering. The principal federal money laundering statutes, 18 U.S.C. 1956 and 1957, outlaw various financial activities that involve the proceeds from other federal crimes. They prohibit:

- domestic laundering the proceeds of these predicate offenses, referred to as "specified unlawful activities;"
- international laundering the proceeds of predicate offenses;
- using the proceeds of predicate offenses to promote further predicate offenses; [210] or
- spending or depositing more than $10,000 of the proceeds of predicate offenses [211].

Offenses under the various paragraphs of 18 U.S.C. 1030 are all money laundering predicate offenses, 18 U.S.C. 1 956(c)(7)(D), 1 957(f)(3). Directly or indirectly they will support a money laundering prosecution as will several of the crimes that may be implicated whenever a paragraph 1030(a)(4) fraud offense is involved: i.e., credit card fraud (18 U.S.C. 1029), and wire fraud (18 U.S.C. 1343).

Financial transactions are defined broadly for money laundering purposes to encompass virtually every possible transfer of wealth, [212] as long as they "in any way or degree affect[] interstate or foreign commerce . . . or . . . involving the use of a financial institution which is engaged in, or the activities of which affect, interstate or foreign commerce in any way or degree," 18 U.S.C. 1 956(c)(4). The proof required to satisfy this "any way or degree" jurisdictional element, even after Lopez, has been characterized as "de minimis," "minimal," "slight," or "incidental." [213]

To establish "promotion" the government need show little more than that the transaction is intended to further the illicit scheme, activity or business [214].

> "The elements necessary to prove a violation of § 1957 are that:
>
> (1) the defendant engage or attempt to engage
> (2) in a monetary transaction
> (3) in criminally derived property that is of a value greater than $10,000
> (4) knowing that the property is derived from unlawful activity, and
> (5) the property is, in fact, derived from 'specified unlawful activity.'" [215]

The predicate offenses are the same as those for section 1956, 18 U.S.C. 1 957(f)(3), the meaning of "monetary transaction" closely tracks that of a "financial transaction" in section 1956, [216] and the definition of monetary transaction includes the jurisdiction component of the offense, that is, that the transaction occurs "in or affecting interstate or foreign commerce," 18 U.S.C. 1

957(f)(1), which requires no more than the de minimis nexus demanded of section 1956 [217]

State Computer Fraud Law. Although the elements vary considerably, most states have explicit statutory prohibitions against computer fraud [218].

Chapter 5

EXTORTIONATE THREATS (18 U.S.C. 1030(A)(7))

Whoever. . . (7) with intent to extort from any person any money or other thing of value, transmits in interstate or foreign commerce any communication containing any threat to cause damage to a protected computer. . . shall be punished as provided in subsection (c) of this section.

Congress added paragraph 1030(a)(7) in 1996 out of concern that "the 'property' protected under existing laws, such as the Hobbs Act, 18 U. S.C. 1951 (interference with commerce by extortion), or 18 U. S.C. 875(d)(interstate communication of threat to injury property of another), does not clearly include the operation of a computer, the data or programs stored in a computer or its peripheral equipment, or the decoding keys to encrypted data," S.Rept. 357 at 12. The paragraph provides that no one shall

- transmit in interstate or foreign commerce
- any communication containing any threat
- to cause damage, (i.e., "any impairment to the integrity or availability of data, a program, a system, or information," (1030(e)(8)))
- to a protected computer, [i.e. one
  - used exclusively for or by the federal government;
  - used exclusively for or by a bank or other financial institution;
  - used in part for or by the federal government where damage would "affect" government use or use of the government's behalf; — used in part for or by a bank or other financial institution where the damage would "affect" use by or on behalf of the institution; or

- used in interstate or foreign commerce or communications
- (1030(e)(2))]

- with the intent to extort money or a thing of value
- from any person [i.e. any individual, firm, association, educational institution, financial institution, government entity, legal or other entity (1030(3)(12))].

Jurisdiction

Paragraph 1030(a)(7) stands on dual jurisdictional footings. First, a successful prosecution is only possible if a threat with intent to extort has been transmitted in interstate or foreign commerce, an element that may be satisfied even in the case of intrastate communications under some circumstances [219]. Second, conviction can only be had if the transmitted threat is directed against a protected computer, i.e., one used in or for interstate or foreign commerce, one used by or for the federal government, or one used by or for a financial institution, 18 U.S.C. 1030(e)(2).

Prior to the 2001 amendment to the definition of "protected computer," a paragraph 1030(a)(7) extortion proscription was said to apply to an extortionate threat initiated overseas but directed at a computer within this country [220]. Then in 2001, Congress noted that the class of computers protected because of their use in interstate or foreign commerce, 18 U.S.C. 1030(e)(2)(B)(2000 ed.), should be understood to "include a computer located outside the United States that is used in a manner than affects interstate or foreign commerce or communication of the United States." [221]. The question arises whether by specifying this particular form of overseas application Congress intended to exclude all others left unmentioned.

Threat of "Damage"

Paragraph 1030(a)(7) proscribes threats to cause computer "damage" and the legislative history describes its reach in terms consistent with the common understanding of the word "damage":

> "New section 1030(a)(7) would close [the] gap in the law and provide penalties for the interstate or international transmission of threats directed against computers and computer systems. This covers any interstate or

international transmission of threats against computers, computer networks, and their data and programs whether the threat is received by mail, a telephone call, electronic mail, or through a computerized massaging service. *Unlawful threats could include interference in any way with the normal operation of the computer or system in question*, such as denying access to authorized users, erasing or corrupting data or programs, slowing down the operation of the computer or system, or encrypting data and then demanding money for the key," S.Rept. 357 at 12 (emphasis added).

Prior to the USA PATRIOT Act amendments, the paragraph did not cover all threats to interfere with the normal operation of protected computers, but only threats to "damage" protected computers and only "damage" as then defined in section 1030, i.e., "any impairment to the integrity or availability of data, a program, a system, or information, that – (A) causes loss aggregating at least $5,000 in value during any 1-year period to one or more individuals; (B) modifies or impairs, or potentially modifies or impairs, the medical examination, diagnosis, treatment, or care of one or more individuals; (C) causes physical injury to any person; or (D) threatens public health or safety," 18 U.S.C. 1030(e)(8)(2000 ed.). The act expanded the damage definition and thus the coverage of the paragraph by reducing the definition to "any impairment to the integrity or availability of data, a program, a system, or information," 18 U.S.C. 1030(e)(8).

Intent

The level of intent required for a violation of paragraph 1030(a)(7) differs from the level used for the fraud provisions of section 1030. Rather than the demand that the offense be committed "knowingly and with an intent to defraud;" offenses under paragraph 103 0(a)(7) must be committed "with the intent to extort." Because the crime is only complete if committed with this intent to extort, it anticipates that the offender will have intended his victim to feel threatened. The paragraph thereby avoids some of the uncertainty that has plagued the threat statutes [222].

Threats

Construction of the threat statutes may provide useful insight, however, into what constitutes a "threat" for purposes of paragraph 1030(a)(7). Although statements of political hyperbole may not always constitute true threats,223 a threat is no less a threat because it is contingent, [224] because the speaker does not intend or is unable to carry it out, [225] because the threat was not directly communicated to the target, [226] or because the language used might be considered cryptic or ambiguous [227]. Whether a particular communication constitutes a threat is a question determined by whether a reasonable person, considering all the circumstances, would regard the communication as a threat [228]. While the jurisdictional element, such as transmission in interstate commerce, must be established, [229] the government need not show the defendant knew that the threat had been transported interstate commerce [230].

Consequences

Penalties & Civil Liability. Violations are punishable by imprisonment for not more than five years (not more than 10 years for second and subsequent offenses) and/or a fine of not more than $250,000, and in cases involving more than $5000 damage or some other qualifying circumstance, victims may claim the advantages of the civil cause of action for damages available under 18 U.S.C. 1030(g) [231]. The general fraud/damage sentencing guideline, U.S.S.G. §2B1.1, applies to violations of paragraph (a)(7).

Other Consequences. Property derived from an extortion offense under paragraph 1030(a)(7) is subject to confiscation, 18 U.S.C. 981 (a)(1)(C), 982(a)(2)(B). Offenders may also be ordered to pay restitution, 18 U.S.C. 3663. Offenses under the paragraph are not considered federal crimes of terrorism, however, 18 U.S.C. 23 32b(g)(5).

Other Crimes

Attempt, Conspiracy and Complicity. The same general observations concerning attempt, conspiracy and aiding and abetting noted with respect to the other paragraphs of 1030(a) apply here. It is a separate crime to attempt to violate paragraph 1030(a)(7), 18 U.S.C. 1030(b). Those who attempt or aid and abet the violation of another are subject to the same penalties as those commit the substantive offense, 18 U.S.C. 1030(c), 2. The same is true of conspiracies except that conspiracy to commit a felony carries a five year maximum of imprisonment, 18 U.S.C. 371.

Hobbs Act. The Hobbs Act, 18 U.S.C. 1951, prohibits extortion that affects commerce. More precisely, among other things, it declares that "Whoever in any way or degree obstructs, delays, or affects commerce or the movement of any article or commodity in commerce, by . . . extortion or attempts or conspires so to do . . . shall be fined under this title or imprisoned not more than twenty years, or both," 18 U.S.C. 1951(a) [232]. For purpose of section 1951, "'extortion' means the obtaining of property from another, with his consent, induced by wrongful use of . . . fear," 18 U.S.C. 1951(b)(2). The government need show only a minimal impact on interstate or foreign commerce to satisfy the jurisdictional element of the Hobbs Act [233].

Facially, paragraph 1030(a)(7) might seem little more than a more specific version of the Hobbs Act: the Hobbs Act prohibits extortionate acquisition of property, generally, in a manner that affects interstate or foreign commerce; while paragraph 1030(a)(7) prohibits extortionate acquisition of property, specifically acquired by a threat to damage computers, in a manner that affects interstate or foreign commerce. But much of section 1030 can be explained by Congress' concern that its purposes could be frustrated by too narrow a definition of "property." In most instances, the fear has been that computer systems or information in computer storage or on computer disks will be considered too intangible to claim the legal protection available to more tangible property. The applicability of the Hobbs Act and of the various "threats with intent to extort" statutes present an additional "property" complication, for they may involve both property under threat and property sought by the extortionist.

There is little question that the act guards against threats to both tangible and intangible property. The cases are replete with the observation that wrongful exploitation of a reasonable fear of economic loss in order to obtain property constitutes extortion for purposes of section 1951 [234]. The case law gives credence to Congress' concern that some may conclude that the Hobbs Act does not always reach cases where the "property" obtained by the extortionist is an intangible benefit rather than tangible property like money [235].

Threat Statutes. Several federal statutes prohibit threats against "property" made with extortionate intent. Here the Hobbs Act puzzle is reversed. Here it is the meaning of the "property" protected from threat that is uncertain; while the meaning of "property" sought by the extortionist is conceded and spacious.

The statutes in question include at a minimum 18 U.S.C. 875 (threats transmitted in interstate commerce), [236] 18 U.S.C. 876 (mailing threatening communications), [237] 18 U.S.C. 877 (mailing threatening communications from a foreign country), [238] and 18 U.S.C. 880 (receipt of the proceeds of extortion) [239] Other than the receipt statute, they are all essentially alike except for their jurisdictional elements. Each prohibits the communication of a threat to injure the property of the addressee or of another conveyed with extortionate intent. Each identifies "money or other thing of value" as the extortionist's objective, and each punishes offenders by imprisonment for not more than two years and/or a fine of not more than $250,000.

As noted earlier, the courts see extraordinary elasticity in the term "thing of value" as used in federal criminal law, [240] but not infrequently are divided over which intangibles may legitimately be considered "property" for purposes of federal criminal statutes [241]. Again even in the case of the "property" statutes, however, the intangibles at issue in computer cases would seem to fall more clearly on the Carpenter "confidential information" side of the line than on the McNally "honest public services" or the Cleveland "unissued license" side.

RICO, Money Laundering, and the Travel Act. Section 1030 is a money laundering predicate offense, 18 U.S.C. 1956(c)(7)(D), 1957(f)(3). Thus, financial transactions involving the proceeds from computer-related extortion that violates paragraph 1030(a)(7) may support a prosecution under 18 U.S.C. 1956 or 1957. Moreover, a violation of paragraph 1030(a)(7) may at the same time offend one of its companions that is a RICO predicate, e.g., the Hobbs Act, 18 U.S.C. 875 (extortion affecting in interstate or foreign commerce), or the Travel Act (extortion is a Travel Act predicate), thereby rising the prospect of a RICO prosecution.

Chapter 6

TRAFFICKING IN COMPUTER ACCESS (18 U.S.C. 1030(A)(6))

> *Whoever . . . (6) knowingly and with intent to defraud traffics (as defined in section 1029) in any password or similar information through which a computer may be accessed without authorization, if -- (A) such trafficking affects interstate or foreign commerce; or (B) such computer is used by or for the Government of the United States . . . shall be punished as provided in subsection (c) of this section.*

Paragraph 1030(a)(6) outlaws misconduct similar to the access device proscriptions of section 1029 [242]. It was enacted to deal with the practice of hackers of posting the passwords of various computer systems on electronic bulletin boards, S.Rept. 99-432 at 13 (1986); H.Rept. 99-612 at 12-3 (1986). Although limited, it provides several distinct advantages.

First, it covers passwords to government computers more clearly than does section 1029.

Second, as something of a lesser included offense to section 1029, it affords the government plea bargain room in a case that it might otherwise be forced to bring under section 1029 or abandon.

Third, it contributes a means of cutting off the practice of publicly posting access to confidential computer systems without imposing severe penalties unless the misconduct persists.

Fourth, it supplies a basis for private enforcement through the civil liability provisions of subsection 1030(g) for misconduct that may be more appropriately addressed by the courts as a private wrong. The elements of the crime are:

- knowingly and with an intent to defraud;
- trafficking in (i.e. "to transfer, or otherwise dispose of, to another, or obtain control of with intent to transfer or dispose of" (18 U.S.C. 1 029(e)(5));
- a computer password or similar computer key; and
- either
  - of a federal computer or
  - in a manner that affects interstate or foreign commerce.

Jurisdiction

Federal jurisdiction exists where the traffic affects interstate or foreign commerce, 18 U.S.C. 1030(a)(6)(A) or where the password or key is to a computer used by or for the Government of the United States, 18 U.S.C. 1030(a)(6)(B). As has been said of other paragraphs and government computers, it is unclear whether the protection of paragraph 1030(a)(6) cloaks legislative and judicial branch computers or is limited to those of the executive branch. The uncertainty is born of the section's care to define the phrase "department or agency of the United States" to include all three branches and its use of that phrase in establishing some crimes, contrasted with its failure to use that phrase in paragraph 1030(a)(6), discussed supra. The explicit reference to overseas application of offenses affecting commerce, 18 U.S.C. 1030(e)(2), without a similar statement concerning government computers may raise further uncertainty. Was the omission an oversight or intended to signal a limitation?

Intent

The intent element is the same as that used in paragraph 1030(a)(4)(fraud), and in the credit card fraud proscriptions of 18 U.S.C. 1029: knowingly and with the intent to defraud, S.Rept. 99-432 at 10 (1986); H.Rept. 99-612 at 12 (1986). The phrase as used in the credit card fraud statute means that the offender is conscious of the natural consequences of his action (i.e., that it likely that someone will be defrauded) and intends that those consequences should occur (i.e., he intends that someone should be defrauded), H.Rept. 98-894 at 16-7 (1984).

Consequences

Penalties. The first offense is punishable by imprisonment for not more than one year and/or a fine of not more than $100,000; subsequent offenses are punishable by imprisonment for not more than 10 years and/or a fine of not more than $250,000, 18 U.S.C. 1030(c)(2); 18 U.S.C. 3571. The general theft/damage sentencing guideline, U.S.S.G. §2B1.1, covers violations of paragraph 1030(a)(6)(traffic in passwords) as it does fraud and damage under paragraphs 1030(a)(4) and 1030(a)(5).

Other Consequences. Proceeds and property traceable to the proceeds of a violation of paragraph 1030(a)(6) trafficking offenses are subject to confiscation, 18 U. S.C. 981 (a)(1)(C), 982(a)(2)(B). Upon conviction, defendants are ordered to pay restitution, 18 U.S.C. 3663A(c)(1)(A)(ii). And offenders may also be subject to a cause of action for damages or injunctive relief, 18 U.S.C. 1030(g).

Other Crimes

The generally applicable provisions dealing with attempt, conspiracy and complicity will apply with equal force in cases involving paragraph 1030(a)(6). Paragraph 1030(a)(6) appears to have few counterparts in federal law, other than the prohibition against trafficking in access devices (credit card fraud) under 18 U.S.C. 1029(a)(2) [243] and the wire fraud provisions of 18 U.S.C. 1343 [244]. Nevertheless, violations of either of these – or of the money laundering proscriptions (18 U.S.C. 1956, 1957) for which section 1030 is a predicate – may provide the foundation for a RICO (18 U.S.C. 1962) prosecution, so that should conduct in violation of paragraph 1030(a)(6) also offend either the mail fraud, credit card fraud or money laundering prohibitions, a criminal breach of RICO may also have occurred. Brokering computer passwords without more may not be the ground upon which a sprawling criminal enterprise might be built, but violations of paragraph 1030(a)(6), with other crimes, might be part of a pattern of criminal activity used to operate such an enterprise.

Chapter 7

COMPUTER ESPIONAGE (18 U.S.C. 1030(A)(1))

Whoever . . . (1) having knowingly accessed a computer without authorization or exceeding authorized access, and by means of such conduct having obtained information that has been determined by the United States Government pursuant to an Executive order or statute to require protection against unauthorized disclosure for reasons of national defense or foreign relations, or any restricted data, as defined in paragraph y of section 11 of the Atomic Energy Act of 1954, with reason to believe that such information so obtained could be used to the injury of the United States, or to the advantage of any foreign nation willfully communicates, delivers, transmits, or causes to be communicated, delivered, or transmitted, or attempts to communicate, deliver, transmit or cause to be communicated, delivered, or transmitted the same to any person not entitled to receive it, or willfully retains the same and fails to deliver it to the officer or employee of the United States entitled to receive it . . . shall be punished as provided in subsection (c) of this section.

Paragraph 1030(a)(1) essentially tracks existing federal espionage laws, 18 U.S.C. 793, 794 and 798, that ban disclosure of information potentially detrimental to our national defense and well being, or more simply laws that outlaw spying [245] The paragraph was enacted as part of the original act and has been amended primarily to more closely track other espionage laws [246] The distinctive feature of paragraph 1030(a)(1) is its merger of elements of espionage and computer abuse [247] Broken down into a simplified version of its constituent elements it bars anyone from:

- either
    - willfully disclosing,

- willfully attempting to disclose, or - willfully failing to return
- classified information concerning national defense, foreign relations or atomic energy with reason to believe that the information either - could to used to injure the United States, or
- could be used to the advantage of the a foreign nation when the information was acquired by unauthorized computer access.

Jurisdiction

The federal government is a creature of the Constitution. It enjoys only those powers that the Constitution grants it, U.S.Const. Amend. IX, X. Since states are primarily responsible for the enactment and enforcement of criminal law, the validity of any federal criminal law depends upon a clear nexus some power that the Constitution vests in the national government. Most of section 1030 represents the execution of Congress' authority to enact laws for the regulation interstate and foreign commerce, for example, U.S.Const. Art.I, §8, cl.3. Paragraph 1030(a)(1), on the other hand, is anchored in the protection of defense and foreign relations of the nation and so jurisdictional ties to interstate or foreign commerce are unnecessary.

Intent

The state of mind element for a breach of paragraph 1030(a)(1) is pegged high. The offender must (1) purposefully transmit or retain information that (2) he has reason to believe could be used to the injure the United States or benefit another country, and (3) that he has obtained through access to a computer that he knows he had no authority to access [248].

Consequences

Penalties and Sentencing Guidelines. Violations are punishable by imprisonment for not more than 10 years (not more than 20 years for second and subsequent offenses) and/or a fine of not more than $250,000, 18 U.S.C. 1030(c)(1), 3571. The general espionage sentencing guideline, U.S.S.G. §2M3.2, applies to violations of paragraph (a)(1) which calls for a base sentencing level of 30 (carrying an initial sentencing range beginning at 8 years imprisonment) and of

35 (an initial sentencing range beginning at 14 years) if top secret information is involved. Since paragraph 1030(a)(1) offenses are federal crimes of terrorism, the minimum sentencing level is 32 and the criminal history category is VI which means the sentencing range begins at 17.5 years imprisonment (and begins at 24.33 years imprisonment if top secret information is involved), U.S.S.G. §3A1.4.

Federal crime of terrorism. Paragraph 1030(a)(1) is a federal crime of terrorism, 18 U. S.C. 23 32b(g)(5)(B). Therefore:

- the applicable statute of limitations is 8 years rather than 5 years, 18 U.S.C. 3286;
- pretrial detention of defendants charged with a violation of paragraph 1030(a)(1) is presumed, 18 U.S.C. 3142;
- conviction carries the prospect of life-time supervision by probation authorities, 18 U.S.C. 3583;
- a paragraph 1030(a)(1) offense is a ground for sentencing enhancement in the case of, or is a predicate offense for: - aggravated identity theft, 18 U.S.C. 1028;
  - RICO, 18 U.S.C. 1961;
  - maritime transportation of terrorists, 18 U.S.C. 2284; and
  - providing material support for terrorist organizations, 18 U.S.C. 2339A.

Other Consequences. Proceeds from a paragraph 1030(a)(1) espionage offense are subject to confiscation, 18 U.S.C. 981(a)(1)(C), 982(a)(2)(B). Upon conviction, defendants are ordered to pay restitution, 18U.S.C.3 663A(c)(1)(A)(ii).

And offenders may also be subject to a cause of action for damages or injunctive relief, 18 U.S.C. 1030(g).

Other Crimes

Espionage prosecutions are not common [249]. And there do not appear to have been any reported cases brought under paragraph 1030(a)(1). The overlap between paragraph 1030(a)(1) and the espionage laws is such, however, that any case prosecutable under paragraph 1030(a)(1) would like also be prosecutable under one or more of the espionage statutes; in fact "the only reported 'espionage' case involving the unauthorized use of computers was prosecuted under §793, the much older, pre-electronic espionage statute and not under § 1030(a)(1)." [250]

Attempt, Conspiracy, and Complicity. Subsection 1030(b) makes it a separate crime to attempt to commit a violation of paragraph 1030(a)(1) punishable to the same extent as the underlying offense, 18 U.S.C. 1030(c). Anyone who commands, counsels, aids or abets a violation of the paragraph assumes is as a principal and is therefore likewise subject to the same penalties, 18 U.S.C. 2. Conspirators to violate paragraph 1030(a)(1) are subject to imprisonment for not more than five years and/or a fine of not more than $250,000, 18 U.S.C. 371, and are each liable for the underlying offense and any other foreseeable crimes committed in furtherance of the conspiracy.

Espionage Offenses. The three espionage statutes themselves share common ground under some circumstances. In general terms, they outlaw gathering and disseminating defense information (18 U.S.C. 793), gathering and disseminating defense information for a foreign country (18 U.S.C. 794), and disclosing classified information concerning government cryptography or communications intelligence (18 U.S.C. 798).

As already noted 18 U.S.C. 793(e) is the generic twin of 1030(a)(1), but section 793 has several other provisions that might also be implicated by a fact pattern sufficient to establish criminal liability under paragraph 1030(a)(1). Section 793 establishes six distinct offenses:

- intruding upon military facilities to gather national defense information (18 U.S.C. 793(a)); [251]
- copying documents containing national defense information (18 U.S.C. 793(b)); [252]
- unlawful receipt of national defense information (18 U.S.C. 793(c)); [253]
- unlawful dissemination of national defense information by a lawful custodian (18 U.S.C. 793(d)); [254]
- unauthorized possession of national defense information (18 U.S.C. 793(e)); [255] and
- negligently losing national defense information (18 U.S.C. 793(f)). [256]

Conspiracy to violate section 793 is likewise punishable by imprisonment for not more than 10 years (not more than 20 years for a subsequent offense) and/or a fine of not more than $250,000, 18 U.S.C. 793(g), and criminal forfeiture of any proceeds derived from the offense, 18 U.S.C. 793(h).

Section 794 essentially subjects transgressions similar to those banned in section 793 to more severe penalties if they involve gathering national defense information for a foreign nation or to injure the United States, [257] particularly if the offense is committed in war time [258]. Conspirators are subject to the same penalties, 18 U.S.C. 794(c), and property derived from a violation or used to facilitate a violation is subject to forfeiture, 18 U.S.C. 794(d).

Section 798 protects military and diplomatic codes and government codebreaking. It proscribes unlawful dissemination of classified information concerning communications intelligence and government cryptography [259]. Violations are punishable by imprisonment for not more than 10 years and/or a fine of not more than $250,000, 18 U.S.C. 798(a), 3571, and the confiscation of any property derived from the offense or used to facilitate its commission, 18 U.S.C. 798(d).

Economic Espionage. The economic espionage prohibition, 18 U.S.C. 1831, outlaws stealing, copying, or unlawfully possessing a trade secret for the benefit of a foreign entity or attempting or conspiring to do so [260].

Offenders face imprisonment for not more than 15 years and a higher fine that permitted for most felonies – not more than $500,000 (not more than $10 million for organizations), id.

RICO and Money Laundering. Violations of Section 793, 794, 798 or 1030 are money laundering predicate offenses, 18 U.S.C. 1956(c)(7)(D). Moreover, violations of paragraph 1030(a)(1) are among the offenses listed in 18 U.S.C. 2332b(g)(5)(B) (federal crimes of terrorism) and are consequently RICO predicate offenses, 18 U.S.C. 1961(1)(G).

APPENDICES

SELECTED BIBLIOGRAPHY

Articles

Friendman & Bissinger, "Infojacking": Crimes on the Information Super Highway, 9 *JOURNAL OF PROPERTY RIGHTS* 2 (1997)

Heymann, Legislating Computer Crime, 34 *HARVARD JOURNAL ON LEGISLATION* 373 (1997)

Kerr, Search and Seizing Computers and Obtaining Electronic Evidence in Criminal Investigations, *COMPUTER CRIME AND INTELLECTUAL PROPERTY SECTION, CRIMINAL DIVISION, UNITED STATES*

DEPARTMENT OF JUSTICE (July, 2002), on [http://www.cybercrime.gov] (Nov.21, 2003)

Levinson & Paetsch, The Computer Fraud and Abuse Act: A Powerful New Way to Protect Information, 19 COMPUTER & INTERNET LAWYERS 11 (Sept. 2002)

Olivenbaum, <CTRL><ALT><DELETE>: Rethinking Federal Computer Crime Legislation, 27 SETON HALL LAW REVIEW 574 (1997)

Sinrod & Reilly, Cyber-Crime: A Practical Approach to the Application of Federal Computer Crime Laws, 16 *SANTA CLARA COMPUTER & HIGH TECHNOLOGY LAW JOURNAL* 177 (2000)

Soma, Banker & Smith, Computer Crime: Substantive Statutes and Technical and Legal Search Considerations, 39 AIR FORCE LAW REVIEW 225 (1996)

United States Department of Justice, *Prosecuting Computer Crimes* (2006)

Notes

Controlling Cyberspace: Applying the Computer Fraud and Abuse Act to the Internet, 12 *SANTA CLARA COMPUTER and HIGH TECHNOLOGY LAW JOURNAL* 403 (1996)

The Limits of Computer Conversion: United States v. Collins, 9 *HARVARD JOURNAL OF LAW & TECHNOLOGY* 205 (1996)

Twenty-Second Survey of White Collar Crime, 44 *AMERICAN CRIMINAL LAW REVIEW* 241 (2007)

18 U.S.C. 1030

(a) Whoever –

(1) having knowingly accessed a computer without authorization or exceeding authorized access, and by means of such conduct having obtained information that has been determined by the United States Government pursuant to an Executive order or statute to require protection against unauthorized disclosure for reasons of national defense or foreign relations, or any restricted data, as defined in paragraph y. of section 11 of the Atomic Energy Act of 1954, with reason to believe that such information so obtained could be used to the injury of the United States, or to the advantage of any foreign nation willfully communicates, delivers, transmits, or causes to be communicated, delivered, or transmitted, or attempts to communicate, deliver, transmit or cause to be communicated, delivered, or transmitted the same to any person not entitled to receive it, or willfully retains the same and fails to deliver it to the officer or employee of the United States entitled to receive it;

(2) intentionally accesses a computer without authorization or exceeds authorized access, and thereby obtains –

(A) information contained in a financial record of a financial institution, or of a card issuer as defined in section 1602(n) of title 15, or contained in a file of a consumer reporting agency on a consumer, as such terms are defined in the Fair Credit Reporting Act (15 U.S.C. 1681 et seq.);

(B) information from any department or agency of the United States; or

(C) information from any protected computer if the conduct involved an interstate or foreign communication;

(3) intentionally, without authorization to access any nonpublic computer of a department or agency of the United States, accesses such a computer of that department or agency that is exclusively for the use of the Government of the

United States or, in the case of a computer not exclusively for such use, is used by or for the Government of the United States and such conduct affects that use by or for the Government of the United States;

(4) knowingly and with intent to defraud, accesses a protected computer without authorization, or exceeds authorized access, and by means of such conduct furthers the intended fraud and obtains anything of value, unless the object of the fraud and the thing obtained consists only of the use of the computer and the value of such use is not more than $5,000 in any 1-year period;

(5)(A)(i) knowingly causes the transmission of a program, information, code, or command, and as a result of such conduct, intentionally causes damage without authorization, to a protected computer;

(ii) intentionally accesses a protected computer without authorization, and as a result of such conduct, recklessly causes damage; or

(iii) intentionally accesses a protected computer without authorization, and as a result of such conduct, causes damage; and

(B) by conduct described in clause (i), (ii), or (iii) of subparagraph (A), caused (or, in the case of an attempted offense, would, if completed, have caused)–

loss to 1 or more persons during any 1-year period (and, for purposes of an investigation, prosecution, or other proceeding brought by the United States only, loss resulting from a related course of conduct affecting 1 or more other protected computers) aggregating at least $5,000 in value;

- (i) the modification or impairment, or potential modification or impairment, of the medical examination, diagnosis, treatment, or care of 1 or more individuals;
- (ii) physical injury to any person;
- (iii) a threat to public health or safety; or
- (iv) damage affecting a computer system used by or for a government entity in furtherance of the administration of justice, national defense, or national security;

(6) knowingly and with intent to defraud traffics (as defined in section 1029) in any password or similar information through which a computer may be accessed without authorization, if--

(A) such trafficking affects interstate or foreign commerce; or

(B) such computer is used by or for the Government of the United States;

(7) with intent to extort from any person any money or other thing of value, transmits in interstate or foreign commerce any communication containing any threat to cause damage to a protected computer;

shall be punished as provided in subsection (c) of this section.

(b) Whoever attempts to commit an offense under subsection (a) of this section shall be punished as provided in subsection (c) of this section.

(c) The punishment for an offense under subsection (a) or (b) of this section is –(1)(A) a fine under this title or imprisonment for not more than ten years, or both, in the case of an offense under subsection (a)(1) of this section which does not occur after a conviction for another offense under this section, or an attempt to commit an offense punishable under this subparagraph; and

(B) a fine under this title or imprisonment for not more than twenty years, or both, in the case of an offense under subsection (a)(1) of this section which occurs after a conviction for another offense under this section, or an attempt to commit an offense punishable under this subparagraph;

(2)(A) except as provided in subparagraph (B), a fine under this title or imprisonment for not more than one year, or both, in the case of an offense under subsection (a)(2), (a)(3), (a)(5)(A)(iii), or (a)(6) of this section which does not occur after a conviction for another offense under this section, or an attempt to commit an offense punishable under this subparagraph;

(B) a fine under this title or imprisonment for not more than 5 years, or both, in the case of an offense under subsection (a)(2), or an attempt to commit an offense punishable under this subparagraph, if–

(i) the offense was committed for purposes of commercial advantage or private financial gain;

(ii) the offense was committed in furtherance of any criminal or tortious act in violation of the Constitution or laws of the United States or of any State; or

(iii) the value of the information obtained exceeds $5,000; and

(C) a fine under this title or imprisonment for not more than ten years, or both, in the case of an offense under subsection (a)(2), (a)(3) or (a)(6) of this section which occurs after a conviction for another offense under this section, or an attempt to commit an offense punishable under this subparagraph;

(3)(A) a fine under this title or imprisonment for not more than five years, or both, in the case of an offense under subsection (a)(4) or (a)(7) of this section which does not occur after a conviction for another offense under this section, or an attempt to commit an offense punishable under this subparagraph; and

(B) a fine under this title or imprisonment for not more than ten years, or both, in the case of an offense under subsection (a)(4) [FN2] (a)(5)(A)(iii), or (a)(7) of this section which occurs after a conviction for another offense under this section, or an attempt to commit an offense punishable under this subparagraph;

(4)(A) except as provided in paragraph (5), a fine under this title, imprisonment for not more than 10 years, or both, in the case of an offense under subsection (a)(5)(A)(i), or an attempt to commit an offense punishable under that subsection;

(B) a fine under this title, imprisonment for not more than 5 years, or both, in the case of an offense under subsection (a)(5)(A)(ii), or an attempt to commit an offense punishable under that subsection;

(C) except as provided in paragraph (5), a fine under this title, imprisonment for not more than 20 years, or both, in the case of an offense under subsection (a)(5)(A)(i) or (a)(5)(A)(ii), or an attempt to commit an offense punishable under either subsection, that occurs after a conviction for another offense under this section; and

(5)(A) if the offender knowingly or recklessly causes or attempts to cause serious bodily injury from conduct in violation of subsection (a)(5)(A)(i), a fine under this title or imprisonment for not more than 20 years, or both; and

(B) if the offender knowingly or recklessly causes or attempts to cause death from conduct in violation of subsection (a)(5)(A)(i), a fine under this title or imprisonment for any term of years or for life, or both.

(d)(1) The United States Secret Service shall, in addition to any other agency having such authority, have the authority to investigate offenses under this section.

The Federal Bureau of Investigation shall have primary authority to investigate offenses under subsection (a)(1) for any cases involving espionage, foreign counterintelligence, information protected against unauthorized disclosure for reasons of national defense or foreign relations, or Restricted Data (as that term is defined in section 1 1y of the Atomic Energy Act of 1954 (42 U.S.C. 20 14(y)), except for offenses affecting the duties of the United States Secret Service pursuant to section 3056(a) of this title.

Such authority shall be exercised in accordance with an agreement which shall be entered into by the Secretary of the Treasury and the Attorney General.

(e) As used in this section –

(1) the term "computer" means an electronic, magnetic, optical, electrochemical, or other high speed data processing device performing logical, arithmetic, or storage functions, and includes any data storage facility or communications facility directly related to or operating in conjunction with such device, but such term does not include an automated typewriter or typesetter, a portable hand held calculator, or other similar device;

(2) the term "protected computer" means a computer –

(A) exclusively for the use of a financial institution or the United States Government, or, in the case of a computer not exclusively for such use, used by or for a financial institution or the United States Government and the conduct constituting the offense affects that use by or for the financial institution or the Government; or

(B) which is used in interstate or foreign commerce or communication, including a computer located outside the United States that is used in a manner that affects interstate or foreign commerce or communication of the United States;

(3) the term "State" includes the District of Columbia, the Commonwealth of Puerto Rico, and any other commonwealth, possession or territory of the United States;

(4) the term "financial institution" means –

(A) an institution, with deposits insured by the Federal Deposit Insurance Corporation;

(B) the Federal Reserve or a member of the Federal Reserve including any Federal Reserve Bank;

(C) a credit union with accounts insured by the National Credit Union Administration;

(D) a member of the Federal home loan bank system and any home loan bank;

(E) any institution of the Farm Credit System under the Farm Credit Act of 1971;

(F) a broker-dealer registered with the Securities and Exchange Commission pursuant to section 15 of the Securities Exchange Act of 1934;

(G) the Securities Investor Protection Corporation;

(H) a branch or agency of a foreign bank (as such terms are defined in paragraphs (1) and (3) of section 1(b) of the International Banking Act of 1978); and

(I) an organization operating under section 25 or section 25(a) of the Federal Reserve Act;

(5) the term "financial record" means information derived from any record held by a financial institution pertaining to a customer's relationship with the financial institution;

(6) the term "exceeds authorized access" means to access a computer with authorization and to use such access to obtain or alter information in the computer that the accesser is not entitled so to obtain or alter;

(7) the term "department of the United States" means the legislative or judicial branch of the Government or one of the executive departments enumerated in section 101 of title 5;

(8) the term "damage" means any impairment to the integrity or availability of data, a program, a system, or information;

(9) the term "government entity" includes the Government of the United States, any State or political subdivision of the United States, any foreign country, and any state, province, municipality, or other political subdivision of a foreign country;

(10) the term "conviction" shall include a conviction under the law of any State for a crime punishable by imprisonment for more than 1 year, an element of which is unauthorized access, or exceeding authorized access, to a computer;

(11) the term "loss" means any reasonable cost to any victim, including the cost of responding to an offense, conducting a damage assessment, and restoring the data, program, system, or information to its condition prior to the offense, and any revenue lost, cost incurred, or other consequential damages incurred because of interruption of service; and

(12) the term "person" means any individual, firm, corporation, educational institution, financial institution, governmental entity, or legal or other entity.

(f) This section does not prohibit any lawfully authorized investigative, protective, or intelligence activity of a law enforcement agency of the United States, a State, or a political subdivision of a State, or of an intelligence agency of the United States.

(g) Any person who suffers damage or loss by reason of a violation of this section may maintain a civil action against the violator to obtain compensatory damages and injunctive relief or other equitable relief. A civil action for a violation of this section may be brought only if the conduct involves 1 of the factors set forth in clause (i), (ii), (iii), (iv), or (v) of subsection (a)(5)(B). Damages for a violation involving only conduct described in subsection (a)(5)(B)(i) are limited to economic damages. No action may be brought under this subsection unless such action is begun within 2 years of the date of the act complained of or the date of the discovery of the damage. No action may be brought under this subsection for the negligent design or manufacture of computer hardware, computer software, or firmware.

(h) The Attorney General and the Secretary of the Treasury shall report to the Congress annually, during the first 3 years following the date of the enactment of this subsection, concerning investigations and prosecutions under subsection (a)(5).

18 U.S.C.1956. Laundering of Monetary Instruments

(a)(1) Whoever, knowing that the property involved in a financial transaction represents the proceeds of some form of unlawful activity, conducts or attempts to conduct such a financial transaction which in fact involves the proceeds of specified unlawful activity –

(A)(i) with the intent to promote the carrying on of specified unlawful activity; or

(ii) with intent to engage in conduct constituting a violation of section 7201 or 7206 of the Internal Revenue Code of 1986; or

(B) knowing that the transaction is designed in whole or in part –

to conceal or disguise the nature, the location, the source, the ownership, or the control of the proceeds of specified unlawful activity; or

(ii) to avoid a transaction reporting requirement under State or Federal law, shall be sentenced to a fine of not more than $500,000 or twice the value of the property involved in the transaction, whichever is greater, or imprisonment for not more than twenty years, or both. For purposes of this paragraph, a financial transaction shall be considered to be one involving the proceeds of specified unlawful activity if it is part of a set of parallel or dependent transactions, any one of which involves the proceeds of specified unlawful activity, and all of which are part of a single plan or arrangement.

(2) Whoever transports, transmits, or transfers, or attempts to transport, transmit, or transfer a monetary instrument or funds from a place in the United States to or through a place outside the United States or to a place in the United States from or through a place outside the United States –

(A) with the intent to promote the carrying on of specified unlawful activity; or

(B)knowing that the monetary instrument or funds involved in the transportation, transmission, or transfer represent the proceeds of some form of unlawful activity and knowing that such transportation, transmission, or transfer is designed in whole or in part –

(i) to conceal or disguise the nature, the location, the source, the ownership, or the control of the proceeds of specified unlawful activity; or

(ii) to avoid a transaction reporting requirement under State or Federal law, shall be sentenced to a fine of not more than $500,000 or twice the value of the monetary instrument or funds involved in the transportation, transmission, or transfer whichever is greater, or imprisonment for not more than twenty years, or both. For the purpose of the offense described in subparagraph (B), the defendant's knowledge may be established by proof that a law enforcement officer represented the matter specified in subparagraph (B) as true, and the defendant's subsequent statements or actions indicate that the defendant believed such representations to be true.

(3) Whoever, with the intent –

(A) to promote the carrying on of specified unlawful activity;

(B) to conceal or disguise the nature, location, source, ownership, or control of property believed to be the proceeds of specified unlawful activity; or

(C) to avoid a transaction reporting requirement under State or Federal law, conducts or attempts to conduct a financial transaction involving property represented to be the proceeds of specified unlawful activity, or property used to conduct or facilitate specified unlawful activity, shall be fined under this title or imprisoned for not more than 20 years, or both. For purposes of this paragraph and paragraph (2), the term "represented" means any representation made by a law enforcement officer or by another person at the direction of, or with the approval of, a Federal official authorized to investigate or prosecute violations of this section.

(b) Penalties. –

(1) In general. – Whoever conducts or attempts to conduct a transaction described in subsection (a)(1) or (a)(3), or section 1957, or a transportation, transmission, or transfer described in subsection (a)(2), is liable to the United States for a civil penalty of not more than the greater of –

(A) the value of the property, funds, or monetary instruments involved in the transaction; or

(B) $10,000.

(2) Jurisdiction over foreign persons. – For purposes of adjudicating an action filed or enforcing a penalty ordered under this section, the district courts shall have jurisdiction over any foreign person, including any financial institution authorized under the laws of a foreign country, against whom the action is brought, if service of process upon the foreign person is made under the Federal Rules of Civil Procedure or the laws of the country in which the foreign person is found, and –

(A) the foreign person commits an offense under subsection (a) involving a financial transaction that occurs in whole or in part in the United States;

(B) the foreign person converts, to his or her own use, property in which the United States has an ownership interest by virtue of the entry of an order of forfeiture by a court of the United States; or

(C) the foreign person is a financial institution that maintains a bank account at a financial institution in the United States.

Court authority over assets. – A court may issue a pretrial restraining order or take any other action necessary to ensure that any bank account or other property held by the defendant in the United States is available to satisfy a judgment under this section.

(4) Federal receiver. –

(A) In general. – A court may appoint a Federal Receiver, in accordance with subparagraph (B) of this paragraph, to collect, marshal, and take custody, control, and possession of all assets of the defendant, wherever located, to satisfy a civil judgment under this subsection, a forfeiture judgment under section 981 or 982, or a criminal sentence under section 1957 or subsection (a) of this section, including an order of restitution to any victim of a specified unlawful activity.

(B) Appointment and authority. – A Federal Receiver described in subparagraph (A)--

(i) may be appointed upon application of a Federal prosecutor or a Federal or State regulator, by the court having jurisdiction over the defendant in the case;

(ii) shall be an officer of the court, and the powers of the Federal Receiver shall include the powers set out in section 754 of title 28, United States Code; and

(iii) shall have standing equivalent to that of a Federal prosecutor for the purpose of submitting requests to obtain information regarding the assets of the defendant –

(I) from the Financial Crimes Enforcement Network of the Department of the Treasury; or

(II) from a foreign country pursuant to a mutual legal assistance treaty, multilateral agreement, or other arrangement for international law enforcement assistance, provided that such requests are in accordance with the policies and procedures of the Attorney General.

(c) As used in this section –

(1) the term "knowing that the property involved in a financial transaction represents the proceeds of some form of unlawful activity" means that the person knew the property involved in the transaction represented proceeds from some form, though not necessarily which form, of activity that constitutes a felony under State, Federal, or foreign law, regardless of whether or not such activity is specified in paragraph (7);

(2) the term "conducts" includes initiating, concluding, or participating in initiating, or concluding a transaction;

(3) the term "transaction" includes a purchase, sale, loan, pledge, gift, transfer, delivery, or other disposition, and with respect to a financial institution includes a deposit, withdrawal, transfer between accounts, exchange of currency, loan, extension of credit, purchase or sale of any stock, bond, certificate of deposit, or other monetary instrument, use of a safe deposit box, or any other payment, transfer, or delivery by, through, or to a financial institution, by whatever means effected;

(4) the term "financial transaction" means (A) a transaction which in any way or degree affects interstate or foreign commerce (i) involving the movement of funds by wire or other means or (ii) involving one or more monetary instruments, or (iii) involving the transfer of title to any real property, vehicle, vessel, or aircraft, or (B) a transaction involving the use of a financial institution which is engaged in, or the activities of which affect, interstate or foreign commerce in any way or degree;

(5) the term "monetary instruments" means (i) coin or currency of the United States or of any other country, travelers' checks, personal checks, bank checks, and money orders, or (ii) investment securities or negotiable instruments, in bearer form or otherwise in such form that title thereto passes upon delivery;

(6) the term "financial institution" includes –

(A) any financial institution, as defined in section 53 12(a)(2) of title 31 ,United States Code, or the regulations promulgated thereunder; and

(B) any foreign bank, as defined in section 1 of the International Banking Act of 1978 (12 U.S.C. 3101);

(7) the term "specified unlawful activity" means –

(A) any act or activity constituting an offense listed in section 1961(1) of this title except an act which is indictable under subchapter II of chapter 53 of title 31;

(B) with respect to a financial transaction occurring in whole or in part in the United States, an offense against a foreign nation involving –

(i) the manufacture, importation, sale, or distribution of a controlled substance (as such term is defined for the purposes of the Controlled Substances Act);

(ii) murder, kidnapping, robbery, extortion, destruction of property by means of explosive or fire, or a crime of violence (as defined in section 16);

(iii) fraud, or any scheme or attempt to defraud, by or against a foreign bank (as defined in paragraph 7 of section 1(b) of the International Banking Act of 1978));

(iv) bribery of a public official, or the misappropriation, theft, or embezzlement of public funds by or for the benefit of a public official;

(v) smuggling or export control violations involving –

(I) an item controlled on the United States Munitions List established under section 38 of the Arms Export Control Act (22 U.S.C. 2778); or

(II) an item controlled under regulations under the Export Administration Regulations (15 C.F.R. Parts 730-774);

(vi) an offense with respect to which the United States would be obligated by a multilateral treaty, either to extradite the alleged offender or to submit the case for prosecution, if the offender were found within the territory of the United States; or

(vii) trafficking in persons, selling or buying of children, sexual exploitation of children, or transporting, recruiting or harboring a person, including a child, for commercial sex acts;

(C) any act or acts constituting a continuing criminal enterprise, as that term is defined in section 408 of the Controlled Substances Act (21 U.S.C. 848);

(D) an offense under section 32 (relating to the destruction of aircraft), section 37 (relating to violence at international airports), section 115 (relating to influencing, impeding, or retaliating against a Federal official by threatening or injuring a family member), section 152 (relating to concealment of assets; false oaths and claims; bribery), section 1 75c (relating to the variola virus), section 215 (relating to commissions or gifts for procuring loans), section 351 (relating to congressional or Cabinet officer assassination), any of sections 500 through 503 (relating to certain counterfeiting offenses), section 513 (relating to securities of States and private entities), section 541 (relating to goods falsely classified), section 542 (relating to entry of goods by means of false statements), section 545 (relating to smuggling goods into the United States), section 549 (relating to removing goods from Customs custody), section 554 (relating to smuggling goods from the United States), section 641 (relating to public money, property, or records), section 656 (relating to theft, embezzlement, or misapplication by bank officer or employee), section 657 (relating to lending, credit, and insurance institutions), section 658 (relating to property mortgaged or pledged to farm credit agencies), section 666 (relating to theft or bribery concerning programs receiving Federal funds), section 793, 794, or 798 (relating to espionage), section 831 (relating to prohibited transactions involving nuclear materials), section 844(f) or (i) (relating to destruction by explosives or fire of Government property or property affecting interstate or foreign commerce), section 875 (relating to interstate communications), section 922(1) (relating to the unlawful importation of firearms), section 924(n) (relating to firearms trafficking), section 956 (relating to conspiracy to kill, kidnap, maim, or injure certain property in a foreign country), section 1005 (relating to fraudulent bank entries), 1006 [FN3] (relating to fraudulent Federal credit institution entries), 1007 (relating to fraudulent Federal Deposit Insurance transactions), 1014 (relating to fraudulent loan or credit applications), section 1030 (relating to computer fraud and abuse), 1032 (relating to concealment of assets from conservator, receiver, or liquidating agent of financial institution), section 1111 (relating to murder), section 1114 (relating to murder of United States law enforcement officials), section 1116 (relating to murder of foreign officials, official guests, or internationally protected persons), section 1201 (relating to kidnaping), section 1203 (relating to hostage taking), section 1361 (relating to willful injury of Government property), section 1363 (relating to destruction of property within the special maritime and territorial jurisdiction), section 1708 (theft from the mail), section 1751 (relating to Presidential assassination), section 2113 or 2114 (relating to bank and postal robbery and theft), section 2280 (relating to violence against maritime navigation), section 2281 (relating to violence against maritime fixed platforms), section 2319 (relating to copyright infringement), section 2320 (relating to trafficking in counterfeit goods and services), section 2332 (relating to terrorist acts abroad against United States nationals), section 2332a (relating to use of weapons of mass destruction), section 2332b (relating to international terrorist acts transcending national boundaries), section 2332g (relating to missile systems designed to destroy aircraft), section 2332h (relating to radiological dispersal devices), section 2339A or 2339B (relating to providing material support to terrorists), section 2339C (relating to financing of terrorism), or section 2339D (relating to receiving military-type training from a foreign terrorist organization) of this title, section 46502 of title 49, United States Code, a felony violation of the Chemical Diversion and Trafficking Act of 1988 (relating to precursor and essential chemicals), section 590 of the Tariff Act of 1930 (19 U.S.C. 1590) (relating to aviation smuggling), section 422 of the Controlled Substances Act (relating to transportation of drug paraphernalia), section 38(c) (relating to criminal violations) of the Arms Export Control Act, section 11 (relating to violations) of the Export Administration Act of 1979, section 206 (relating to penalties) of the International Emergency Economic Powers Act, section 16 (relating to offenses and punishment) of the Trading with the Enemy Act, any felony violation of section 15 of the Food Stamp Act of 1977 [7 U.S.C.A. § 2024] (relating to food stamp fraud) involving a quantity of coupons having a value of not less than $5,000, any violation of section 543(a)(1) of the Housing Act of 1949 42 U.S.C.A. § 1490s(a)(1)] (relating to equity skimming), any felony violation of the Foreign Agents Registration Act of 1938, any felony violation of the Foreign Corrupt Practices Act, or section 92 of the Atomic Energy Act of 1954 (42 U.S.C. 2122) (relating to prohibitions governing atomic weapons)

ENVIRONMENTAL CRIMES

(E) a felony violation of the Federal Water Pollution Control Act (33 U.S.C. 1251 et seq.), the Ocean Dumping Act (33 U.S.C. 1401 et seq.), the Act to Prevent Pollution from Ships (33 U.S.C. 1901 et seq.), the Safe Drinking Water Act (42 U.S.C. 300f et seq.), or the Resources Conservation and Recovery Act (42 U.S.C. 6901 et seq.); or

(F) any act or activity constituting an offense involving a Federal health care offense;

(8) the term "State" includes a State of the United States, the District of Columbia, and any commonwealth, territory, or possession of the United States.

(d) Nothing in this section shall supersede any provision of Federal, State, or other law imposing criminal penalties or affording civil remedies in addition to those provided for in this section.

(e) Violations of this section may be investigated by such components of the Department of Justice as the Attorney General may direct, and by such components of the Department of the Treasury as the Secretary of the Treasury may direct, as appropriate, and, with respect to offenses over which the Department of Homeland Security has jurisdiction, by such components of the Department of Homeland Security as the Secretary of Homeland Security may direct, and, with respect to offenses over which the United States Postal Service has jurisdiction, by the Postal Service. Such authority of the Secretary of the Treasury, the Secretary of Homeland Security, and the Postal Service shall be exercised in accordance with an agreement which shall be entered into by the Secretary of the Treasury, the Secretary of Homeland Security, the Postal Service, and the Attorney General. Violations of this section involving offenses described in paragraph (c)(7)(E) may be investigated by such components of the Department of Justice as the Attorney General may direct, and the National Enforcement Investigations Center of the Environmental Protection Agency.

(f) There is extraterritorial jurisdiction over the conduct prohibited by this section if –

(1) the conduct is by a United States citizen or, in the case of a non-United States citizen, the conduct occurs in part in the United States; and

(2) the transaction or series of related transactions involves funds or monetary instruments of a value exceeding $10,000.

(g) Notice of conviction of financial institutions. – If any financial institution or any officer, director, or employee of any financial institution has been found guilty of an offense under this section, section 1957 or 1960 of this title, or section 5322 or 5324 of title 31, the Attorney General shall provide written notice of such fact to the appropriate regulatory agency for the financial institution.

(h) Any person who conspires to commit any offense defined in this section or section 1957 shall be subject to the same penalties as those prescribed for the offense the commission of which was the object of the conspiracy.

(i) Venue.– (1) Except as provided in paragraph (2), a prosecution for an offense under this section or section 1957 may be brought in –

(A)any district in which the financial or monetary transaction is conducted; or

(B) any district where a prosecution for the underlying specified unlawful activity could be brought, if the defendant participated in the transfer of the proceeds of the specified unlawful activity from that district to the district where the financial or monetary transaction is conducted.

(2) A prosecution for an attempt or conspiracy offense under this section or section 1957 may be brought in the district where venue would lie for the completed offense under paragraph (1), or in any other district where an act in furtherance of the attempt or conspiracy took place (3) For purposes of this section, a transfer of funds from 1 place to another, by wire or any other means, shall constitute a single, continuing transaction. Any person who conducts (as that term is defined in subsection (c)(2)) any portion of the transaction may be charged in any district in which the transaction takes place.

RICO Predicate Offenses ("Racketeering Activities"). 18 U.S.C. 1961(1)

(A) any act or threat involving murder, kidnapping, gambling, arson, robbery, bribery, extortion, dealing in obscene matter, or dealing in a controlled substance or listed chemical (as defined in section 102 of the Controlled Substances Act), which is chargeable under State law and punishable by imprisonment for more than one year;

(B) any act which is indictable under any of the following provisions of title 18, United States Code: Section 201 (bribery), section 224 (sports bribery), sections 471, 472, and 473 (counterfeiting), section 659 (theft from interstate shipment) if the act indictable under section 659 is felonious, section 664 (embezzlement from pension and welfare funds), sections 891-894 (extortionate credit transactions), section 1028 (fraud and related activity in connection with identification documents), section 1029 (fraud and related activity in connection with access devices), section 1084 (the transmission of gambling information), section 1341 (mail fraud), section 1343 (wire fraud), section 1344 (financial institution fraud), section 1425 (the procurement of citizenship or nationalization unlawfully), section 1426 (the reproduction of naturalization or citizenship papers), section 1427 (the sale of naturalization or citizenship papers), sections 1461-1465 (obscene matter), section 1503 (obstruction of justice), section 1510 (obstruction of criminal investigations), section 1511 (the obstruction of State or local law enforcement), section 1512 (tampering with a witness, victim, or an informant), section 1513 (retaliating against a witness, victim, or an informant), section 1542 (false statement in application and use of passport), section 1543 (forgery or false use of passport), section 1544 (misuse of passport), section 1546 (fraud and misuse of visas, permits, and other documents), sections 1581-1592 (peonage, slavery, and trafficking in persons), section 1951 (interference with commerce, robbery, or extortion), section 1952 (racketeering), section 1953 (interstate transportation of wagering paraphernalia), section 1954 (unlawful welfare fund payments), section 1955 (the prohibition of illegal gambling businesses), section 1956 (the laundering of monetary instruments), section 1957 (engaging in monetary transactions in property derived from specified unlawful activity), section 1958 (use of interstate commerce facilities in the commission of murder-for-hire), section 1960 (illegal money transmitters), sections 2251, 225 1A, 2252, and 2260 (sexual exploitation of children), sections 2312 and 2313 (interstate transportation of stolen motor vehicles), sections 2314 and 2315 (interstate transportation of stolen property), section 2318 (trafficking in counterfeit labels for phonorecords, computer programs or computer program documentation or packaging and copies of motion pictures or other audiovisual works), section 2319 (criminal infringement of a copyright), section 231 9A (unauthorized fixation of and trafficking in sound recordings and music videos of live musical performances), section 2320 (trafficking in goods or services bearing counterfeit marks), section 2321 (trafficking in certain motor vehicles or motor vehicle parts), sections 2341-2346 (trafficking in contraband cigarettes), sections 242 1-24 (white slave traffic), sections 175-178 (biological weapons) , sections 229-229F (chemical weapons), section 831 (nuclear materials),

(C) any act which is indictable under title 29, United States Code, section 186 (dealing with restrictions on payments and loans to labor organizations) or section 501(c) (embezzlement from union funds),

(D) any offense involving fraud connected with a case under title 11 (except a case under section 157 of this title), fraud in the sale of securities, or the felonious manufacture, importation, receiving, concealment, buying, selling, or otherwise dealing in a controlled substance or listed chemical (as defined in section 102 of the Controlled Substances Act), punishable under any law of the United States,

(E) any act which is indictable under the Currency and Foreign Transactions Reporting Act,

(F) any act which is indictable under the Immigration and Nationality Act, section 274 (bringing in and harboring certain aliens), section 277 (aiding or assisting certain aliens to enter the United States), or section 278 (importation of alien for immoral purpose) if the act indictable under such section of such Act was committed for the purpose of financial gain, or

(G) any act that is indictable under any provision listed in section 2332b(g)(5)(B).

FEDERAL CRIMES OF TERRORISM

18 U.S.C. 2332b(g)(5)(B)

(i) section 32 (destruction of aircraft or aircraft facilities), 37 (violence at international airports), 81 (arson within special maritime and territorial jurisdiction), 175 or 1 75b (biological weapons), 1 75c (variola virus), 229 (chemical weapons), subsection (a), (b), (c), or (d) of section 351 (congressional, cabinet, and Supreme Court assassination and kidnaping), 831 (nuclear materials), 832 (participation in nuclear and weapons of mass destruction threats to the United States) [FN1] 842(m) or (n) (plastic explosives), 844(f)(2) or (3) (arson and bombing of Government property risking or causing death), 844(i) (arson and bombing of property used in interstate commerce), 93 0(c) (killing or attempted killing during an attack on a Federal facility with a dangerous weapon), 956(a)(1) (conspiracy to murder, kidnap, or maim persons abroad), 1030(a)(1) (protection of computers), 1030(a)(5)(A)(i) resulting in damage as defined in 1030(a)(5)(B)(ii) through (v) (protection of computers), 1114 (killing or attempted killing of officers and employees of the United States), 1116 (murder or manslaughter of foreign officials, official guests, or internationally protected persons), 1203 (hostage taking), 1361 (government property or contracts), 1362 (destruction of communication lines, stations, or systems), 1363 (injury to buildings or property within special maritime and territorial jurisdiction of the United States), 1366(a) (destruction of an energy facility), 1751(a), (b), (c), or (d) (Presidential and Presidential staff assassination and kidnaping), 1992 (terrorist attacks and other acts of violence against railroad carriers and against mass transportation systems on land, on water, or through the air), 2155 (destruction of national defense materials, premises, or utilities), 2156 (national defense material, premises, or utilities), 2280 (violence against maritime navigation), 2281 (violence against maritime fixed platforms), 2332 (certain homicides and other violence against United States nationals occurring outside of the United States), 2332a (use of weapons of mass destruction), 2332b (acts of terrorism transcending national boundaries), 2332f (bombing of public places and facilities), 2332g (missile systems designed to destroy aircraft), 2332h (radiological dispersal devices), 2339 (harboring terrorists), 2339A (providing material support to terrorists), 2339B (providing material support to terrorist organizations), 2339C (financing of terrorism), 2339D (military-type training from a foreign terrorist organization), or 2340A (torture) of this title;

(ii) sections 92 (prohibitions governing atomic weapons) or 236 (sabotage of nuclear facilities or fuel) of the Atomic Energy Act of 1954 (42 U.S.C. 2122 or 2284);

(iii) section 46502 (aircraft piracy), the second sentence of section 46504 (assault on a flight crew with a dangerous weapon), section 465 05(b)(3) or (c) (explosive or incendiary devices, or endangerment of human life by means of weapons, on aircraft), section 46506 if homicide or attempted homicide is involved (application of certain criminal laws to acts on aircraft), or section 60123(b) (destruction of interstate gas or hazardous liquid pipeline facility) of title 49; or

(iv) section 1010A of the Controlled Substances Import and Export Act (narco-terrorism).

18 U.S.C. 1992

(a) Whoever, in a circumstance described in subsection (c), knowingly and without lawful authority or permission – (1) wrecks, derails, sets fire to, or disables railroad on-track equipment or a mass transportation vehicle; . . . (4) sets fire to, undermines, makes unworkable, unusable, or hazardous to work on or use . . . in, upon, or near any – (A) tunnel, bridge, viaduct, trestle, track, electromagnetic guideway, signal, station, depot, warehouse, terminal, or any other way, structure, property, or appurtenance used in the operation of, or in support of the operation of, a railroad carrier, and with intent to, or knowing or having reason to know, such activity would likely, derail, disable, or wreck railroad on-track equipment; or (B) garage, terminal, structure, track, electromagnetic guideway, supply, or facility used in the operation of, or in support of the operation of, a mass transportation vehicle, and with intent to, or knowing or having reason to know, such activity would likely, derail, disable, or wreck a mass transportation vehicle used, operated, or employed by a mass transportation provider; (5) removes an appurtenance from, damages, or otherwise impairs the operation of a railroad signal system or mass transportation signal or dispatching system, including a train control system, centralized dispatching system, or highway-railroad grade crossing warning signal; (6) with intent to endanger the safety of any person, or with a reckless disregard for the safety of human life, interferes with, disables, or incapacitates any dispatcher, driver, captain, locomotive engineer, railroad conductor, or other person while the person is employed in dispatching, operating, controlling, or maintaining railroad on-track equipment or a mass transportation vehicle; (7) commits an act . . . with the intent to cause death or serious bodily injury to any person who is on property described in subparagraph (A) or (B) of paragraph (4); (8) surveils, photographs, videotapes, diagrams, or otherwise collects information with the intent to plan or assist in planning any of the acts described in paragraphs (1) through (6); (9) conveys false information, knowing the information to be false, concerning an attempt or alleged attempt to engage in a violation of this subsection; or (10) attempts, threatens, or conspires to engage in any violation of any of paragraphs (1) through (9), shall be fined under this title or imprisoned not more than 20 years, or both, and if the offense results in the death of any person, shall be imprisoned for any term of years or for life, or subject to death, except in the case of a violation of paragraph (8), (9), or (10).

(b) Aggravated offense.– Whoever commits an offense under subsection (a) of this section in a circumstance in which – (1) the railroad on-track equipment or mass transportation vehicle was carrying a passenger or employee at the time of the offense; (2) the railroad on-track equipment or mass transportation vehicle was carrying high-level radioactive waste or spent nuclear fuel at the time of the offense; or (3) the offense was committed with the intent to endanger the safety of any person, or with a reckless disregard for the safety of any person, and the railroad on-track equipment or mass transportation vehicle was carrying a hazardous material at the time of the offense that – (A) was required to be placarded under subpart F of part 172 of title 49, Code of Federal Regulations; and (B) is identified as class number 3, 4, 5, 6.1, or 8 and packing group I or packing group II, or class number 1, 2, or 7 under the hazardous materials table of section 172.101 of title 49, Code of Federal Regulations, shall be fined under this title or imprisoned for any term of years or life, or both, and if the offense resulted in the death of any person, the person may be sentenced to death.

(c) Circumstances required for offense.– A circumstance referred to in subsection (a) is any of the following: (1) Any of the conduct required for the offense is, or, in the case of an attempt, threat, or conspiracy to engage in conduct, the conduct required for the completed offense would be, engaged in, on, against, or affecting a mass transportation provider, or a railroad carrier engaged in interstate or foreign commerce. (2) Any person travels or communicates across a State line in order to commit the offense, or transports materials across a State line in aid of the commission of the offense.

(d) Definitions.– In this section . . . (7) the term 'mass transportation' has the meaning given to that term in section 5302(a)(7) of title 49, except that the term includes intercity bus transportation school bus, charter, and sightseeing transportation and passenger vessel as that term is defined in section 2 101(22) of title 46, United States Code; (8) the term 'on-track equipment' means a carriage or other contrivance that runs on rails or electromagnetic guideways; (9) the term 'railroad on-track equipment' means a train, locomotive, tender, motor unit, freight or passenger car, or other on-track equipment used, operated, or employed by a railroad carrier; (10) the term 'railroad' has the meaning given to that term in chapter 201 of title 49; (11) the term 'railroad carrier' has the meaning given to that term in chapter 201 of title 49; (12) the term 'serious bodily injury' has the meaning given to that term in section 1365; (13) the term 'spent nuclear fuel' has the meaning given to that term in section 2(23) of the Nuclear Waste Policy Act of 1982 (42 U.S.C. 10101(23) . . .(1 6) the term 'vehicle' means any carriage or other contrivance used, or capable of being used, as a means of transportation on land, on water, or through the air.

REFERENCES

[1] The full text of 18 U.S.C. 1030 is appended. Earlier versions of this report appeared under the title, *Computer Fraud and Abuse: An Overview of 18 U.S. C. 1030 and Related Federal Criminal Laws.*

[2] Congressional inquiry began no later than 1976, S. Comm. on Government Operations, *Problems Associated with Computer Technology in Federal Programs and Private Industry – Computer Abuses*, 94th Cong., 2d Sess. (1976)(Comm.Print). Hearings were held in successive Congresses thereafter until passage of the original version of section 1030 as part of the Comprehensive Crime Control Act of 1984, P.L. 98-473, 98 Stat. 2190; *see e.g., Federal Computer Systems Protection Act: Hearings Before the Subcomm. on Criminal Laws and Procedures of the Senate Comm. on the Judiciary*, 95th Cong., 2d Sess.(1978); *S.240, the Computer Systems Protection Act of 1979: Hearings Before the Subcomm. on Criminal Justice of the Senate Comm. on the Judiciary*, 96th Cong., 2d Sess.(1980); *Federal Computer System Protection Act, H.R. 3970: Hearings Before the House Comm. on the Judiciary*, 97th Cong., 2d Sess.(1982); *Computer Crime: Hearings Before the House Comm. on the Judiciary*, 98th Cong., 1st Sess. (1983).

Refurbishing of the original 1984 legislation occurred in 1986, 1988, 1989, 1990, 1994, and 1996: P.L. 99-474, 100 Stat. 1213; P.L. 100-690, 102 Stat. 4404; P.L. 10 1-73, 103 Stat. 502; P.L. 101-647, 104 Stat. 4831; P.L. 103-322, 108 Stat. 2097; P.L. 104-294, 110 Stat. 3491. Most recently, both the USA PATRIOT Act, P.L. 107-56, 115 Stat. 272 (2001) and the Department of Homeland Security Act, P.L. 107-296, 116 Stat. 2135 (2002) amended provisions of section 1030.

For a chronological history of the act up to but not including the 1996 amendments, see Adams, *Controlling Cyberspace: Applying the Computer*

Fraud and Abuse Act to the Internet, 12 SANTA CLARA COMPUTER & HIGH TECHNOLOGY LAW JOURNAL 403 (1996). For a general description of the validity and application of this act, see ; Buchman, *Validity, Construction, and Application of Computer Fraud and Abuse Act*, 174 ALR Fed. 101 (2004); Berkowitz, *Computer Security and Privacy: The Third Wave of Property Law*, 33 COLORADO LAWYER 57 (Feb. 2004); *Prosecuting Intellectual Property Crimes*, COMPUTER CRIME AND INTELLECTUAL PROPERTY SECTION, CRIMINAL DIVISION, UNITED STATES DEPARTMENT OF JUSTICE [(2006)](*DoJ Computer Crime)*, available on February 22, 2008 at [http://www.cybercrime.gov/ipmanual/index.html].

[3] For a discussion of these and similar matters see, *Twenty-Second Survey of White Collar Crime: Computer Crimes*, 44 AMERICAN CRIMINAL LAW REVIEW 313 (2007); CRS Report RL3 1919, *Remedies Available to Victims of Identity Theft*; CRS Report 95-804, *Obscenity and Indecency: Constitutional Principles and Federal Statutes*; CRS Report 9 5-406, *Child Pornography: Constitutional Principles and Federal*; CRS Report 97-6 19, *Internet Gambling: Overview of Federal Criminal Law*; Kerr, *The Fourth Amendment and New Technologies: Constitutional Myths and the Case for Caution*, 102 MICHIGAN LAW REVIEW 802 (2004); *DoJ Computer Crime*.

[4] The Department of Justice maintains a website which provides a list of prosecutions for "computer intrusion", commonly known as "hacking,"as well as cases, statutes and other documentation associated with cybercrime, available on February 22, 2008 at [http://www.cybercrime.gov].

[5] "(e) As used in this section . . . (1) the term 'computer' means an electronic, magnetic, optical, electrochemical, or other high speed data processing device performing logical, arithmetic, or storage functions, and includes any data storage facility or communications facility directly related to or operating in conjunction with such device, but such term does not include an automated typewriter or typesetter, a portable hand held calculator, or other similar device," 18 U.S.C. 1030(e)(1).

[6] "(e) As used in this section . . . (7) the term 'department of the United States' means the legislative or judicial branch of the Government or one of the executive departments enumerated in section 101 of title 5," 18 U.S.C. 1030(e)(7)

[7] "The Executive departments are: The Department of State. The Department of the Treasury. The Department of Defense. The Department of Justice. The Department of the Interior. The Department of Agriculture. The

Department of Commerce. The Department of Labor. The Department of Health and Human Services. The Department of Housing and Urban Development. The Department of Transportation. The Department of Energy. The Department of Education. The Department of Veterans Affairs. The Department of Homeland Security." 5 U.S.C. 101.

[8] *United States v. Bowman*, 260 U.S. 94, 98 (1922)("But the same rule of [territorial] interpretation should not be applied to criminal statutes which. . . are enacted because of the right of the Government to defend itself against obstruction, or fraud wherever perpetrated, especially if committed by its own citizens, officers or agents. Some such offenses . . . are such that to limit their locus to the strictly territorial jurisdiction would be greatly to curtail the scope and usefulness of the statute and leave open a large immunity for frauds as easily committed by citizens on the high seas and in foreign countries as at home. In such cases, Congress has not thought it necessary to make specific provision in the law that the locus shall include the high seas and foreign countries, but allows it to be inferred from the nature of the offense").

[9] *Ford v. United States*, 273 U.S. 589 (1927)("The principle that a man who outside a country wilfully puts in motion a force to take effect in it is answerable at the place where the evil is done, is recognized in the criminal jurisprudence of all countries").

[10] *United States v. Ivanov*, 175 F.Supp.2d 367, 374-75 (D. Conn. 2001).

[11] Id. at 374 ("the Committee specifically noted its concern that the statute as it existed prior to the 1996 amendments did not cover 'computers used in foreign communications or commerce, despite the fact hackers are often foreign-based.' The Committee cited two specific cases in which foreign-based hackers had infiltrated computer systems in the United States, as examples of the kind of situation the amendments were intended to address. . . . Congress has the power to apply its statutes extraterritorially, and in the case of 18 U.S.C 1030, it has clearly manifested its intention to do so"), quoting and citing, S.Rept. 104-357, at 4-5 (1996).

[12] The amendment appears as paragraph 8 14(d)(1) of the USA PATRIOT Act, P.L. 107-56, 115 Stat. 384 (2001).

[13] By virtue of 18 U.S.C. 3571, all felonies are subject to fines of not more than the greater of $250,000 or twice the amount of the pecuniary gain or loss associated with the offense, unless provisions applicable to a specific crime either call for a higher maximum fine or were enacted subsequent to 1984 when the general provisions of section 3571 became effective.

Most federal criminal statutes give the impression that offenders may be sentenced to imprisonment, to a fine or to both imprisonment and a fine. This may be something of an illusion in most serious federal cases. Federal sentencing is influenced by sentencing guidelines that calibrate sentencing levels beneath the maximum terms established in the statute for a particular offense, according to the circumstances of the crime and the offender, see generally, CRS Report RL3 2846, *How the Federal Sentencing Guidelines Work: Two Examples*. While a sentence in compliance with the Guidelines is no longer mandatory, *United States v. Booker*, 543 U.S. 220, 226-27 (2005), federal courts must begin the sentencing process by calculating the applicable sentencing range under the Guidelines and justify any departure from that range, *Gall v. United States*, 128 S.Ct. 586, 596 (2007).

[14] See generally *Juvenile Delinquents and Federal Criminal Law: The Federal Juvenile Delinquency Act and Related Matters*, CRS Rept. RL3 0822.

[15] In 1994, Congress amended the paragraph to emphasize that trespassing upon computers used part-time for the government required a showing that government use was "adversely" affected rather than merely affected, P.L.103-322, 108 Stat. 2099. Concerned that it might suggest that trespassing could be beneficial, Congress repealed the 1994 amendment in 1996 when it also made changes to make it clear that a person "permitted to access publicly available Government computers . . . may still be convicted under (a)(3) for accessing without authority any nonpublic Federal Government computer" and that a person may be convicted under paragraph (a)(3) for access that affects the use of a computer employed on behalf of the government regardless of whether the computer is actually operated by the government or is merely operated for the government, P.L. 104-294, 110 Stat. 3491; S.Rept. 104-357 at 9 (1996).

[16] Olivenbaum, *<CTRL><ALT><DELETE>: Rethinking Federal Computer Crime Legislation*, 27 SETON HALL LAW REVIEW 574, 600-1 (1997); *United States v. Rice, aff'g w/o published op.*, 961 F.2d 211 (4th Cir. 1992), subsequent motion for correction of sentence, 815 F.Supp. 158 (W.D.N.C. 1993).

Rice is a curious case. The unpublished opinion indicates that Rice, a long time Internal Revenue Service (IRS) agent, hacked into the IRS computers at the behest of a drug dealer and disclosed to the dealer the status of an IRS investigation of the dealer; the agent also advised the dealer on means of evading forfeiture of his house. For this he was convicted of conspiracy to launder his friend's drug profits (18 U.S.C. 1 956(a)(1)(b)(i)), conspiracy to defraud the United States of forfeitable property (26 U.S.C. 7214), computer fraud , i.e., accessing the computer system of a government agency without authority (18 U.S.C. 1030(a)(3)), and unauthorized disclosure of confidential information (18 U.S.C. 1905)(sometimes known as the Trade Secrets Act). The court did not address the apparent conflict between the conviction and the legislative history of paragraph 1030(a)(3) indicating that the paragraph does not govern cases of an employee hacking into the computer systems of his own agency. See also *Brownlee v. Dyncorp*, 349 F.3d 1343, 1346 (Fed Cir. 2003) (noting that the guilty plea to charges under § 1030(a)(3) of the employee of a government contractor resulting from the employee's entering false data regarding hours worked into the government computer system)

[17] *DoJ Computer Crime*, at 21 ("Section 11030(a)(3) is not charged often, and few cases interpret it. This lack is probably because section 1030(a)(2) applies in many of the same cases in which section 1030(a)(3) could be charged. In such cases, section 1030(a)(2) may be the preferred charge because statutory sentencing enhancements sometimes allow section 1030(a)(2) to be charged as a felony on the first offense. A violation of section 1030(a)(3), on the other hand, is only a misdemeanor for a first offense").

[18] Throughout this report, "other crimes" refers to closely related crimes. In any given case, a defendant charged under one of the paragraphs of 1030(a) may also be charged under one or more of these other federal companion statutes. As long as there is at least one element required for conviction of one but not the other, a defendant guilty of violating one or more of the various paragraphs of section 1030 may also be held liable for one or more related offenses, see e.g. *United States v. Czubinski*, 106 F.3d 1069 (1st Cir. 1997) (convictions under 18 U.S.C. 1343 (wire fraud) and 18 U.S.C. 1030(a)(4) (computer fraud) overturned for other reasons); United States v. Petersen, 98 F.3d 502 (9th Cir. 1996) (upholding a sentence imposed for convictions under 18 U.S.C. 371 (conspiracy), 18 U.S.C. 1343 (wire fraud), and 18 U.S.C. 1030(a)(4) (computer fraud)).

[19] Subsection 1030(b) states in its entirety, "Whoever attempts to commit an offense under subsection (a) of this section shall be punished as provided in subsection (c) of this section."

[20] *United States v. Neal*, 78 F.3d 901, 906 (4th Cir. 1996); *United States v. Adams*, 305 F. 3d 30, 34 (1st Cir. 2002).

[21] See e.g., 18 U.S.C. 1951 (attempt to obstruct interstate commerce by extortion or robbery); 18 U.S.C. 794 (attempt to communicate national

defense information to a foreign government). There are separate attempt offenses in over 130 sections of title 18 alone: e.g., 18 U.S.C. 32, 33, 37, 112, 115, 152.

[22] *United States v. Resendiz-Ponce*, 127 S.Ct. 782, 787 (2007); *United States v. Kenyon*, 481 F.3d 1054, 1069 (8th Cir. 2007); *United States v. Coté*, 504 F.3d 682, 687 (7th Cir. 2007); *United States v. Ballinger*, 395 F.3d 1218, 1238 n.8 (11th Cir. 2005)

[23] *United States v. Spurlock*, 495 F.3d 1011, 1014 (8th Cir. 2007); *United States v. Yost*, 479 F.3d 815, 819 (1 1th Cir. 2007); *United States v. Rankin*, 487 F.3d 229, 231 (5th Cir. 2007); *United States v. Munro*, 394 F.3d 865, 869 (10th Cir. 2005).

[24] *United States v. Lucas*, 499 F.3d 769, 780 (8th Cir. 2007); *United States v. Wesley*, 417 F.3d 612, 618 (6th Cir. 2005); *United States v. Bellew*, 369 F.3d 450, 453 n.2 (5th Cir. 2004).

[25] *United States v. Turner*, 501 F.3d 59, 68 (1st Cir. 2007); *Doe v. Smith*, 470 F.3d 331, 344 (7th Cir. 2006); *United States v. Murrell*, 368 F.3d 1283, 1286 (11th Cir. 2004).

[26] *United States v. Barnes*, 230 F.3d 311, 315 (7th Cir. 2000); *United States v. Plummer*, 221 F.3d 1298, 1303 (11th Cir. 2000); *United States v. Ramirez*, 348 F.3d. 1175, 1180 (10th Cir. 2003); *United States v. Spenser*, 439 F.3d 905, 915 (8th Cir. 2006).

[27] *United States v. Goetzke*, 494 F.3d 1231, 1237 (9th Cir. 2007)("To constitute a substantial step, a defendant's actions must cross the line between preparation and attempt by unequivocally demonstrating that the crime will take place unless interrupted by independent circumstances"); *United Stats v. Turner*, 501 F.3d 59, 68 (1st Cir. 2007)("While 'mere preparation' does not constitute a substantial step, a defendant does not have to get very far along the line toward ultimate commission of the object crime in order to commit the attempt offense"); *United States v. Ramirez*, 348 F.3d. 1175, 1180 (10th Cir. 2003)(noting that a substantial step "must be an act adapted to, approximating, and which in the ordinary and likely course of things will result in, the commission of the particular crime. A substantial step is an appreciable fragment of a crime and an action of such substantiality that, unless frustrated, the crime would have occurred. The step must be strongly corroborative of the firmness of the defendant's criminal intent and must unequivocally mark the defendant's acts as criminal. It should evidence commitment to the criminal venture")(citing *United States v. Smith*, 264 F.3d 1012, 1016 (10th Cir. 2001)).

[28] "If two or more persons conspire . . . to commit any offense against the United States . . . or any agency thereof in any manner or for any purpose, and one or more of such persons do any act to effect the object of the conspiracy, each shall be fined under this title or imprisoned not more than five years, or both.

"If, however, the offense, the commission of which is the object of the conspiracy, is a misdemeanor only, the punishment for such conspiracy shall not exceed the maximum punishment provided for such misdemeanor," 18 U.S.C. 371; see generally, *Twenty-Second Survey of White Collar Crime: Federal Criminal Conspiracy*, 44 AMERICAN CRIMINAL LAW REVIEW 523 (2007); *Developments in the Law – Criminal Conspiracy*, 72 HARVARD LAW REVIEW 920 (1959).

[29] *United States v. Shellef*, 507 F.3d 82, 105 (2d Cir. 2007); *United States v. Spano*, 421 F.3d 599, 603 (7th Cir. 2005); *United States v. Tucker*, 376 F.3d 236, 238 (4th Cir. 2004)

[30] *Pinkerton v. United States*, 328 U.S. 640, 645-48 (1946); *United States v. Parkes*, 497 F.3d 220, 232 (2d Cir. 2007)(Under *Pinkerton v. United States*, "a defendant who does not directly commit a substantive offense may nevertheless be liable if the commission of the offense by a co-conspirator in furtherance of the conspiracy was reasonably foreseeable to the defendant as a consequence of their criminal agreement"); *United States v. Moran*, 493 F.3d 1002, 1009-110 (9th Cir. 2007); *United States v. Roberson*, 474 F.3d 432, 433 (7th Cir. 2007).

[31] "(a) Whoever commits an offense against the United States or aids, abets, counsels, commands, induces or procures its commission, is punishable as a principal.

"(b) Whoever willfully causes an act to be done which if directly performed by him or another would be an offense against the United States, is punishable as a principal," 18 U.S.C. 2; see generally, Blakey & Roddy, *Reflections on* Reves v. Ernst & Young*: Meaning and Impact on Substantive, Accessory, Aiding Abetting and Conspiracy Liability Under RICO*, 33 AMERICAN CRIMINAL LAW REVIEW 1345, 1385-418 (1996); see also, *United States v. Yakou*, 393 F.3d 231, 242 (D.C. Cir. 2005)("The statute typically applies to any criminal statute unless Congress specifically carves out an exception that precludes aiding and abetting liability, and it long has been established that a person can be convicted of aiding and abetting another person's violation of a statute even if it would be impossible to convict the aider and abettor as a principal")(citations omitted).

[32] *United States v. Pando Franco*, 503 F.3d 389, 394 (5th Cir. 2007)("to prove the crime of aiding and abetting, the government must establish that the substantive offense occurred and that the defendant (1) associated with a criminal venture, (2) purposefully participated in the crime, and (3) sought by action for it to succeed"); *United States v. Lopez*, 484 F.3d 1186, 1199 (9th Cir. 2007); *United States v. Garcia-Carrasquillo*, 483 F.3d 124, 130 (1st Cir. 2007).

[33] *Id.* at 130; *United States v. Sutcliffe*, 505 F.3d 944, 959 (9th Cir. 2007); *United States v. Gardner*, 488 F.3d 700, 713 (6th Cir. 2007).

[34] *United States v. Washington*, 106 F.3d 983, 1004-5 (D.C.Cir. 1997)("if the principal had actually attempted to commit a crime but had failed, the aider and abettor would be charged with the same offense as the principal (attempt to commit the crime)"). See also *United States v. Villanueva*, 408 F.3d 193, 202 (5th Cir. 2005) (finding defendant guilty of aiding and abetting an attempted crime); *United States v. Gardner*, 488 F.3d 700, 711 (6th Cir. 2007)(aiding and abetting attempted possession of cocaine).

[35] The definition of "protected computer" in section 1037 defers to the definition in 1030(e)(2(B), which covers any computer "used in interstate or foreign commerce or communication" and implicates any computer connected to the Internet.

[36] CAN-SPAM is discussed more in depth *infra* in relation to section 1030(a)(4) on Computer Fraud.

[37] Most states have statutes that outlaw simple computer trespassing: ALA.CODE § 1 3A-8- 102; ALASKA STAT. §11.46.484; ARIZ.REV.STAT.ANN. §13-2316; ARK.CODE ANN. §5-41- 104; CAL. PENAL CODE §502; COLO.REV.STAT.ANN. § 18-5.5-102; CONN.GEN.STAT.ANN. §53a-25 1; DEL.CODE ANN. tit. 11 §932; FLA.STAT.ANN. §815.06; HAWAII REV.STAT. §708- 895.5 to 708-895.7; IDAHO CODE § 18-2202; ILL.COMP. STAT.ANN. ch.720 §5/16D-3; IND.CODE ANN. §35-43-2-3; IOWA CODE ANN. §716.6B, 702.1A; KAN. STAT.ANN. §21- 3755(d); KY.REV.STAT.ANN. §434.853; LA.REV.STAT.ANN. § 14:73.7; ME.REV.STAT.ANN. tit.17-A §432; MD.CRIM.CODE ANN. §7-302; MASS.GEN. LAWS ANN. ch.266 §120F; MINN.STAT.ANN. §609.891; MISS.CODE ANN. §97-45-9; MO.ANN.STAT. §569.099; MONT.CODE ANN. §45-6-311; NEB.REV.STAT. §28-1347; NEV. REV.STAT. §205.4765; N.H. REV.STAT.ANN. §638:17; N.J. STAT.ANN. §2C:20-25; N.Y. PENAL LAW § 156.10; N.C.GEN. STAT. §14-454; N.D.CENT. CODE §12.1-06.1-08; OHIO REV. CODE ANN. §2913.04(B); OKLA.STAT.ANN. tit.21

§1953; ORE.REV.STAT. §164.377; PA. STAT.ANN. tit.18 §§7611, 7615; R.I.GEN. LAWS §11-52-3; S.C.CODE ANN. §16-16-20(4); S.D.COD.LAWS §43-43B-1; TENN.CODE ANN. §39-14-602; TEX.PENAL CODE ANN. §33.02; UTAH CODE ANN. §76-6- 703; VT.STAT. ANN. tit.13 §4102; WASH. REV.CODE ANN. §9A.52.110; W.VA.CODE ANN. §61-3C-5; WIS. STAT.ANN. §943.70; WYO. STAT. §6-3-504. Analysis of state law is generally beyond the scope of this report. Members of the military may also incur liability under the Uniform Code of Military Justice for various forms of computer abuse. See United States v. Wiest, 59 M.J. 276 (Ct. App. Armed Forces 2004) (reversing lower court on other grounds) in which an Air Force Academy cadet was convicted of a violation of Article 134 of the Uniform Code of Military Justice, for accessing a protected computer without authorization and recklessly damaging a computer in violation of 18 U.S.C. § 1030(a)(5)(B)). See also, United States v. Mervine, 26 M.J. 482 (1 988)(suggesting that various computer crimes might be charged under Article 134, the general article: "Though not specifically mentioned in this chapter, all disorders and neglects to the prejudice of good order and discipline in the armed forces, all conduct of a nature to bring discredit upon the armed forces, and crimes and offenses not capital, of which persons subject to this chapter may be guilty, shall be taken cognizance of by a general, special, or summary court-martial, according to the nature and degree of the offense, and shall be punished at the discretion of that court").

[38] "(a) Offense.– Except as provided in subsection (c) of this section whoever – (1) intentionally accesses without authorization a facility through which an electronic communication service is provided; or (2) intentionally exceeds an authorization to access that facility; and thereby obtains, alters, or prevents authorized access to a wire or electronic communication while it is in electronic storage in such system shall be punished as provided in subsection (b) of this section.

Punishment.– The punishment for an offense under subsection (a) of this section is– (1) if the offense is committed for purposes of commercial advantage, malicious destruction or damage, or private commercial gain or in furtherance of any criminal or tortious act in violation of the Constitution or laws of the United States or any State– (A) a fine under this title or imprisonment for not more than 5 years, or both, in the case of a first offense under this subparagraph; and (B) a fine under this title or imprisonment for not more than 10 years, or both, for any subsequent offense under this subparagraph; and (2) in any other case– (A) a fine under this title or imprisonment for not more than 1 year or both, in the case of a first offense under this paragraph; and (B) a fine under this title or imprisonment for not more than 5 years, or both, in the case of an offense under this subparagraph that occurs after a conviction of another offense under this section.

Exceptions.–Subsection (a) of this section does not apply with respect to conduct authorized– (1) by the person or entity providing a wire or electronic communications service; (2) by a user of that service with respect to a communication of or intended for that user; or (3) in section 2703, 2704 or 2518 of this title," 18 U.S.C. 2701.

The provisions of 18 U.S.C. 2511 (wiretapping) may apply to the unlawful interception of e-mail transmissions while in transit and 18 U.S.C. 2701 may apply to the unlawful seizure of stored e-mail. Offenses under §2511 are punishable by imprisonment for not more than 5 years as well, 18 U.S.C. 2511(4).

[39] "(a) Except as otherwise provided in this section, whoever, in any matter within the jurisdiction of the executive, legislative, or judicial branch of the Government of the United States, knowingly and willfully – (1) falsifies, conceals, or covers up by any trick, scheme, or device a material fact; (2) makes any materially false, fictitious, or fraudulent statement or representation; or (3) makes or uses any false writing or document knowing the same to contain any materially false, fictitious, or fraudulent statement or entry; shall be fined under this title or imprisoned not more than 5 years or, if the offense involves international or domestic terrorism (as defined in section 2331), imprisoned not more than 8 years, or both. "(b) Subsection (a) does not apply to a party to a judicial proceeding, or that party's counsel, for statements, representations, writings or documents submitted by such party or counsel to a judge or magistrate in that proceeding.

"(c) With respect to any matter within the jurisdiction of the legislative branch, subsection (a) shall apply only to – (1) administrative matters, including a claim for payment, a matter related to the procurement of property or services, personnel or employment practices, or support services, or a document required by law, rule, or regulation to be submitted to the Congress or any office or officer within the legislative branch; or (2) any investigation or review, conducted pursuant to the authority of any committee, subcommittee, commission or office of the Congress, consistent with applicable rules of the House or Senate," 18 U.S.C. 1001; see generally, *Twenty-Second Survey of White Collar Crime: False Statements and False Claims*, 44 AMERICAN CRIMINAL LAW REVIEW 491 (2007).

[40] "Whoever falsely assumes or pretends to be an officer or employee acting under the authority of the United States or any department, agency or officer thereof, and acts as such, or in such pretended character demands or obtains any money, paper, document, or thing of value, shall be fined under this title or imprisoned not more than three years, or both," 18 U.S.C. 912.

[41] Olivenbaum, *<CTRL><ALT><DELETE>: Rethinking Federal Computer Legislation*, 27 SETON HALL LAW REVIEW 574, 600 (1997)(citing an instance from the infancy of section 1030 where a hacker was indicted under the false statement, 18 U.S.C. 1001, and wire fraud, 18 U.S.C. 1343, statute. The case ended when the defendant pled to a misdemeanor fraud charge). No comparable prosecutions followed and so the author's thesis remains unproven.

[42] *Hubbard v. United States*, 514 U.S. 695 (1 995)(overturning an earlier holding that section 1001 applied to false statements made to federal courts and to Congress as well as those made to the executive branch)(superceded by statute, P.L. 104-292, 110 Stat. 3459 (1996)(the modification preserved the exception that it did not apply "to a party to a judicial proceeding, or that party's counsel, for statements, representations, writings or documents submitted by such party or counsel to a judge or magistrate in that proceeding.")(section 1001(b)); United States v. Gaudin, 515 U.S. 509 (1 995)(holding that materiality of the false statement, as an element of section 1001, is a question for the jury to decide).

[43] *United States v. Gaudin*, 515 U.S. 506, 509 (1995)("the statement must have a natural tendency to influence, or be capable of influencing the decision of the decisonmaking body to which it was addressed"); *United States v. Baker*, 200 F.3d 558, 561 (8th Cir. 2000) ("The materiality inquiry focuses on whether the false statement had a natural tendency to influence or was capable of influencing the government agency or official"). *United States v. Mitchell*, 388 F.3d 1139, 1143 (8th Cir. 2004) (noting that a false statement must have "a natural tendency to influence or is capable of influencing the government agency or official" and that "[m]ateriality does not require proof that the government actually relied on the statement.").

[44] *United States v. Collins*, 56 F.3d 1416 (D.C.Cir. 1995) and *United States v. Czubinski*, 106 F.3d 1069 (1st Cir. 1997), overturned convictions under 18 U.S.C. 641 (theft of government property), and 18 U.S.C. 1343 (wire fraud) and 1030(a)(4)(computer fraud) respectively, on the ground that the prosecution had failed to show any adverse impact upon the government caused by the defendant's unauthorized access of government computer files.

[45] "Whoever . . . pretends to be an officer . . . acting under the authority of the United States . . . *and acts as such, or in such pretended character demands or obtains any . . . thing of value,*" 18 U.S.C. 912 (emphasis added).

[46] "The term 'card issuer' means any person who issues a credit card, or the agent of such person with respect to such card," 15 U.S.C. 1602(n).

"The term 'person' means a natural person or an organization. The term 'organization' means a corporation, government or governmental subdivision or agency, trust, estate, partnership, cooperative, or association. The term 'credit card' means any card, plate, coupon book or other credit device existing for the purpose of obtaining money, property, labor, or services on credit. The term 'credit' means the right granted by a creditor to a debtor to defer payment of debt or to incur debt and defer its payment.

"The term 'creditor' refers only to a person who both (1) regularly extends, whether in connection with loans, sales of property or services, or otherwise, consumer credit which is payable by agreement in more than four installments or for which the payment of a finance charge is or may be required, and (2) is the person to whom the debt arising from the consumer credit transaction is initially payable on the face of the evidence of indebtedness or, if there is no such evidence of indebtedness, by agreement. Notwithstanding the preceding sentence, in the case of an open-end credit plan involving a credit card, the card issuer and any person who honors the credit card and offers a discount which is a finance charge are creditors . . ." 15 U.S.C. 1602(d), (c),(k), (e), and (f), respectively.

[47] "The term 'file', when used in connection with information on any consumer, means all of the information on that consumer recorded and retained by a consumer reporting agency regardless of how the information is stored.

"The term 'consumer reporting agency' means any person which, for monetary fees, dues, or on a cooperative nonprofit basis, regularly engages in whole or in part in the practice of assembling or evaluating consumer credit information or other information on consumers for the purpose of furnishing consumer reports to third parties, and which uses any means or facility of interstate commerce for the purpose of preparing or furnishing consumer reports.

"The term 'consumer' means an individual," 15 U.S.C. 1681a(g), (f) and (c), respectively.

[48] "To prove a violation of [subparagraph 1030](a)(2)(C), the Government must show that the defendant (1) intentionally accessed a computer, (2) without authorization (or exceeding authorized access), (3) and thereby

obtained information from any protected computer if the conduct involved interstate or foreign communication," *United States v. Willis*, 476 F.3d 1121, 1125 (1 0th Cir. 2007); *Ticketmaster L.L. C. v. RMG Technologies, Inc.*, 507 F.Supp.2d. 1096, 1113 (C.D. Cal. 2007). The third element of the offense becomes – "thereby obtained information from a financial institution" or "thereby obtained information from a federal agency" – when the violation involves subparagraphs 1030(a)(2)(A)(relating to obtaining financial institution information) or 1030(a)(2)(B)(relating to obtaining federal agency information).

[49] H.Rept. 99-612 at 9-10 (1986); see also, S.Rept. 99-432 at 5-6 (1986)("such conduct. . .must have been the person's conscious objective"); *Butera & Andrews v. IBM, Inc.*, 456 F.Supp. 104, 110 (D.D.C. 2006)

[50] *United States v. Willis*, 476 F.3d 1121, 1125 (10th Cir. 2007).

[51] *Shurgard Storage Centers v. Safeguard Self Storage*, 119 F. Supp. 2d 1121 (W.D. Wash. 2000) (unauthorized access found when employees used their access to benefit a competitor); YourNetDating v. Mitchell, 88 F. Supp. 2d 870 (N.D. Ill. 2000) (former employee found to be exceeding authorized access because he used his access codes to divert users from his ex-employers website). *Southwest Airlines Co. v. Farecase, Inc.*, 318 F.Supp.2d 435, 439-40 (N.D. Tex. 2004)(use of software to gather fare information from airline's website in spite of "no scrapping" warnings constitutes a violation of paragraph 1030(a)(2)).

[52] *Role Models America v. Jones*, 305 F. Supp. 2d 564, 566-7 (D.Md.2004) (the court rejected the claim that a university "accessed" a computer when a high school employee sent them information from the high school computer). For additional analysis on the meanings of these terms, see generally, Orin S. Kerr, *Cybercrime 's Scope: Interpreting "Access" & "Authorization" in Computer Misuse Statutes*, 78 N.Y.U.L.R. 1596 (2003).

[53] Yet it may not require a great deal more than a paragraph 1030(a)(3) prosecution, since merely viewing material on a computer screen has been found to constitute obtaining information for purposes of paragraph 1030(a)(2), *Healthcare Advocates, Inc. v. Harding, Early, Follmer & Frailey*, 497 F.Supp.2d 927, 648 (E.D. Pa. 2007), citing S.Rept. 99-432 at 6-7 (1986)

[54] "As used in this section . . . (2) the term 'protected computer' means a computer . . . (B) which is used in interstate or foreign commerce or communication, *including a computer located outside the Untied States that is used in a manner that affects interstate or foreign commerce or*

communication of the United States," 18 U.S.C. 1030(e)(2)(B)(language of the amendment in italics)

[55] 4 NIMMER & NIMMER, NIMMER ON COPYRIGHT §15.01 n.1.2 (1997) (emphasis added)("*Apparently*, the phrase 'commercial advantage or private financial gain' is intended as the equivalent of 'for profit'"); 1 FISHMAN & MCKENNA, WIRETAPPING AND EAVESDROPPING, SECOND EDITION §4:29 *b.* (1995) comparing, *Stockler v. Garratt*, 893 F.2d 856 (6th Cir. 1990), with, *By-Product Corp. v. Armen-Berry Co.*, 668 F.2d 956 (7th Cir. 1982)(in disagreement over whether an offender must act upon his or her criminal or tortious purpose after recording a conversation to which they are a party or where one party to the conversation has consented to the recording).

[56] At one time, federal sentencing courts were essentially bound by the Guidelines, 18 U.S.C. 3553(b)(1). *Booker* changed that, see *United States v. Booker*, 543 U.S. 220, 245 (2005)("We answer the question of remedy by finding the provision of the federal sentencing statute that makes the Guidelines mandatory, 18 U.S.C.A. 3553(b)(1)(Supp. 2004), incompatible with today's constitutional holding. We conclude that this provision must be severed and excised. . . ."). Now, federal sentencing courts must begin by identifying the appropriate sentencing range under the Guidelines, but enjoy discretion to make justifiable reasonable departures, *Gall v. United States*, 128 S.Ct. 586, 596-97 (2007).

[57] S.Rept. 98-225, at 50-2 (1983).

[58] U.S.S.G. §§1B1.1, 8A1.2.

[59] *Id.*

[60] U.S.S.G. ch.5, pt.A, §5E1.2, ch.8 pt.C.

[61] *United States v. Willis*, 476 F.3d 1121, 1127-128 (10th Cir. 2007), citing U.S.S.G. §2B 1.1 (b)(1)(C). Paragraph 2B 1.1 (b)(1) instructs a sentencing court to increase to an offender's offense level under section 2B 1.1 according to the amount of the loss associated with the offense. In Mr. Willis's case, the loss was more than $10,000 but less than $30,000. Had it been more than $30,000 but less than $70,000 an increase of 6 would have been appropriate. The enhancements are calibrated to account for losses from $5,000 (add 2) to more than $4 million (add 30).

[62] *Id.* at 1128. U.S.S.G. §2B1.1(b)(10)(C)(i) states, "If the offense involved . . .(C)(i) the unauthorized transfer or use of any means of identification unlawfully to produce or obtain any other means of identification . . . increase by 2 levels." Mr. Willis had given Ms. Fischer a username and

password that gave her unauthorized access to a financial information database, which she used in an identity theft scheme.

[63] *Id.* U.S.S.G. §3b1 .3 states, "If the defendant abused a position of public or private trust, or used a special skill, in a manner that significantly facilitated the commission or concealment of the offense, increase by 2 levels." Mr. Willis acquired in his position as supervisor in a debt collection agency the username and password which he had then passed on to his accomplice. Although not implicated here, the special skill enhancement often implicated in the offenses outlawed in the various paragraphs of 18 U.S.C. 1030.

[64] *Id.* Mr. Willis had a fairly extensive record of previous convictions. Had he been a first time offender, his criminal history category would have been I and his sentencing range at an offense level of 14 would have been 15 to 21 months, U.S.S.G. Ch.5, Pt. A (Sentencing Table).

[65] 18 U.S.C. 981(a)(1)(C), 982(a)(2)(B). Criminal forfeiture is accomplished following the criminal prosecution of the property owner, 18 U.S.C. 982. Civil forfeiture is accomplished through an in rem proceeding directed against the property itself, 18 U.S.C. 983. See generally, *Crime and Forfeiture*, CRS Rept. 97-139.

[66] See generally, *Restitution in Federal Criminal Cases*, CRS Rept. RL34138.

[67] E.g., *United States v. Phillips*, 477 F.3d 215, 224-25 (5th Cir. 2007)(restitution ordered for violations of paragraph 1030(a)(5)(damage of a protected computer)).

[68] "(b) The [restitution] order may require that such defendant – (1) in the case of an offense resulting in damage to or loss or destruction of property of a victim of the offense – (A) return the property to the owner of the property or someone designated by the owner; or (B) if return of the property under subparagraph (A) is impossible, impractical, or inadequate, pay an amount equal to the greater of – (i) the value of the property on the date of the damage, loss, or destruction, or (ii) the value of the property on the date of sentencing, less the value (as of the date the property is returned) of any part of the property that is returned," 18 U.S.C. 3663(b)(1).

[69] 18 U.S.C. 3663(a)(3).

[70] 18 U.S.C. 3563(b)(2), 3583(d)(3). Supervised release is a period of supervision to be served after an individual is released from prison, 18 U.S.C. 3583(a).

[71] "Any person who suffers damage or loss by reason of a violation of this section may maintain a civil action against the violator to obtain

compensatory damages and injunctive relief or other equitable relief. A civil action for a violation of this section may be brought only if the conduct involves 1 of the factors set forth in clause (i), (ii), (iii), (iv), or (v) of subsection (a)(5)(B). . . ." 18 U.S.C. 1030(g).

[72] 18 U.S.C. 1030(a)(5)(B).

[73] *Theofel v. Farey-Jones*, 359 F.3d 1066, 1078 n.5 (9th Cir. 2004)("Defendants argue that subsection (a)(5)(A) prescribes the act's only civil offenses. But subsection (g) applies to any violation of 'this section' and, while the offenses must involve one of the five factors in (a)(5)(B), it need not be one of three offenses in (a)(5)(A)"); *Bansal v. Russ*, 513 F.Supp.2d 264, 278 n. 11 (E.D. Pa. 2007); *America Online, Inc. v. National Health Care Discount, Inc.*, 174 F.Supp.2d 890, 899 (N.D. Iowa 2001); cf., *P.C. Yonkers, Inc. v. Celebrations, the Party, and Seasonal Superstore, LLC*, 428 F.3d 504, 512 (3d Cir. 2005) (reaching the same conclusion in the context of a suit under paragraph (a)(4)); *Nexans Wires S.A. v. Sark-USA, Inc.*, 319 F.Supp.2d 468, 472 (S.D.N.Y. 2004)(holding that plaintiffs must satisfy the 1030(a)(5)(B) threshold for each of several claims under 1030(a)(2), (a)(4), and (a)(5)).

[74] The courts have concluded that the civil remedies under the statute are available to third parties. The court in *Theofel v. Farey-Jones*, 359 F.3d 1066, 1078 (9th Cir. 2004), emphasized that the statute extends a civil remedy to *any* individual who suffers loss or damage, thus "[i]ndividuals other than the computer's owner may be proximately harmed by unauthorized access, particularly if they have rights to data stored on it."

[75] The Dictionary Act, for example, defines the term to include "corporations, associations, firms, partnerships, societies, and joint stock companies, as well as individuals," unless the context suggests otherwise, 1 U.S.C. 1.

[76] "Whoever . . . (7) with intent to extort from any *person, firm, association, educational institution, financial institution, government entity, or other legal entity*, any money or other thing of value . . ." 18 U.S.C. 1030(a)(7)(emphasis added)(the 2002 amendments struck out "firm, association, educational institution, financial institution, government entity, or other legal entity").

[77] *Pinkerton v. United States*, 328 U.S. 640, 645-48 (1946); *United States v. Parkes*, 497 F.3d 220, 232 (2d Cir. 2007)(Under *Pinkerton v. United States*, "a defendant who does not directly commit a substantive offense may nevertheless be liable if the commission of the offense by a co-conspirator in furtherance of the conspiracy was reasonably foreseeable to the defendant as a consequence of their criminal agreement"); *United States v. Moran*, 493 F.3d 1002, 1009-110 (9th Cir. 2007); *United States v. Roberson*, 474 F.3d 432, 433 (7th Cir. 2007).

[78] *United States v. Willis*, 476 F.3d 1121, 1125 (10th Cir. 2007).

[79] See, *United States v. Jordan*, 316 F.3d 1215, 1223-224 (1 1th Cir. 2003)(noting the indictment of a sheriff, for improper use of access to the FBI's NCIC database, under paragraph 1030(a)(2), 18 U.S.C. 2 (aiding and abetting), 371 (conspiracy), and 641 (theft of federal property); the overlap between section 1030 and federal laws that prohibit the theft of intangible property under various circumstances is discussed at greater length in the examination of paragraph 1030(a)(4)(fraud), *infra*.

[80] See, *Konop v. Hawaiian Airlines, Inc.*, 302 F.3d 868, 875-80 (9th Cir. 2002)(discussing the application of 18 U.S.C. 2511 and 2701 to a case of unauthorized access to a secure website). See also *Motorola Credit Corp. v. Uzan*, 388 F.3d 39, 44 (2d Cir. 2004) (discussing civil suit claiming violations of sections 1030, 2511, and 2701).

[81] *United States v. Kammersell*, 196 F.3d 1137, 1138-140 (10th Cir. 1999)(a threat communicated between two computers in Utah involved interstate communications because the communication was forwarded by way of AOL's server in Virginia); *United States v. Trotter*, 478 F.3d 918, 921, 922 (8th Cir. 2007)("As both the means to engage in commerce and the method by which transactions occur, the Internet is an instrumentality and channel of interstate commerce . . . [O]nce the computer is used in interstate commerce, Congress has the power to protect it"); *United States v. Sutcliffe*, 505 F.3d 944, 953 (9th Cir. 2007); *United States v. Mitra*, 405 F.3d 492, 496 (7th Cir. 2005).

[82] "[T]he term 'protected computer' means a computer – (A) exclusively for the use of a financial institution or the United States Government, or, in the case of a computer not exclusively for such use, used by or for a financial institution or the United States Government and the conduct constituting the offense affects that use by or for the financial institution or the Government; or (B) which is used in interstate or foreign commerce or communication, *including a computer located outside the United States that is used in a manner that affects interstate or foreign commerce or communication of the United States*," 18 U.S.C. 1030(e)(2)(language added in the USA PATRIOT Act in italics).

[83] "Whoever transports, transmits, or transfers in interstate or foreign commerce any goods, wares, merchandise, securities or money, of the value of $5,000 or more, knowing the same to have been stolen, converted or taken by fraud; or "Whoever, having devised or intending to devise any scheme or artifice to defraud, or for obtaining money or property by means of false or fraudulent pretenses, representations, or promises, transports or

causes to be transported, or induces any person or persons to travel in, or to be transported in interstate or foreign commerce in the execution or concealment of a scheme or artifice to defraud that person or those persons of money or property having a value of $5,000 or more; or

"Whoever, with unlawful or fraudulent intent, transports in interstate or foreign commerce any falsely made, forged, altered, or counterfeited securities or tax stamps, knowing the same to have been falsely made, forged, altered, or counterfeited; or

"Whoever, with unlawful or fraudulent intent, transports in interstate or foreign commerce any traveler's check bearing a forged countersignature; or

"Whoever, with unlawful or fraudulent intent, transports in interstate or foreign commerce, any tool, implement, or thing used or fitted to be used in falsely making, forging, altering, or counterfeiting any security or tax stamps, or any part thereof—

"Shall be fined under this title or imprisoned not more than ten years, or both..." 18 U.S.C. 2314.

[84] *Dowling v. United States*, 473 U.S. 207, 216 (1985). *Dowling* involved the transportation of bootleg phonograph records which were not themselves stolen.

[85] *United States v. Brown*, 925 F.2d 1301, 1305-309 (10th Cir. 1991); *United States v. Lyons*, 992 F.2d 1029, 1033 (10th Cir. 1993)("In *Brown*, we applied the Supreme Court's decision in *Dowling v. United States*, 474 U.S. 207 (1985) to computer software, and held that the intangible intellectual property of a computer program standing alone cannot constitute goods, wares or merchandise within the meaning of 18 U.S.C. 2314. The fact that Mr. Lyons stole the software in conjunction with the theft of tangible hardware distinguishes this case from Brown. Brown recognizes that the theft of intangible intellectual property in conjunction with the theft of tangible property falls within the ambit of §2314. Unlike the present case, there was no evidence in Brown that [the] defendant was involved in the physical theft or transportation of stolen tangible property"); United States v. Martin, 228 F.3d 1, 14 (1st Cir. 2000)(section 2314 applies "when there has been some tangible item taken, however insignificant or valueless it may be, absent the intangible component"). But see United States v. Riggs, 739 F. Supp 414, 420 (N.D. Ill. 1990) which found the electronic transfer of proprietary information to be covered by this statute ("if the information in [the plaintiff's] text file had been affixed to a floppy disk, or printed out on a computer printer, then [defendant's] transfer of that information across state lines would clearly constitute the transfer of goods, wares, or

merchandise within the meaning of § 2314. This court sees no reason to hold differently simply because [defendant] stored the information inside computers instead of printing it out on paper. In either case, the information is in a transferrable, accessible, even salable form."). See also United States v. Farraj, 142 F. Supp. 2d 484 (S.D.N.Y. 200 1)(the court disagreed with Brown and the 10th Circuit line of cases, and instead determined "the view most closely analogous to Second Circuit doctrine is that which holds that the transfer of electronic documents via the internet across state lines does fall within the purview of § 2314").

If section 2314 does apply to a given case, then section 2315 that prohibits receipt of stolen property may also be implicated.

[86] "Whoever embezzles, steals, or unlawfully takes, carries away, or conceals, or by fraud or deception obtains from any pipeline system, railroad car . . . with intent to convert to his own use any goods or chattels moving as or which are a part of or which constitute an interstate or foreign shipment of freight, express, or other property; or

"Whoever buys or receives or has in his possession any such goods or chattels "Whoever, with unlawful or fraudulent intent, transports in interstate or foreign commerce, any tool, implement, or thing used or fitted to be used in falsely making, forging, altering, or counterfeiting any security or tax stamps, or any part thereof –

"Shall be fined under this title or imprisoned not more than ten years, or both. ." 18 U.S.C. 2314.

[87] "Whoever embezzles, steals, purloins, or knowingly converts to his use or the use of another, or without authority, sells, conveys or disposes of any record, voucher, money, or thing of value of the United States or of any department or agency thereof, or any property made or being made under contract for the United States or any department or agency thereof; or

"Whoever receives, conceals, or retains the same with intent to convert it to his use or gain, knowing it to have been embezzled, stolen, purloined or converted –

"Shall be fined under this title or imprisoned not more than ten years, or both; but if the value of such property in the aggregate, combining amounts from all the counts for which the defendant is convicted in a single case, does not exceed the sum of $1,000, he shall be fined under this title or imprisoned not more than one year, or both."

"The word 'value' means face, par, or market value, or cost price, either wholesale or retail, whichever is greater," 18 U.S.C. 641.

[88] See e.g., *United States v. Forman*, 180 F.3d 766, 767-68 (6th Cir. 1 999)(information from a confidential government report concerning a criminal investigation); United States *v. Collins*, 56 F.3d 1416, 1419-420 (D.C.Cir. 1 995)(computer time and storage); *United States v. Martzkin*, 14 F.3d 1014, 1018-21 (4th Cir. 1994)(bids on government contracts); *United States v. Jeter*, 775 F.2d 670, 680 (6th Cir. 1 985)(information as to matters occurring before a federal grand jury); *United States v. Girard*, 601 F.2d 69, 70-1 (2d Cir. 1979) (identity of government undercover agents); *United States v. Lambert*, 446 F.Supp. 890, 892-95 (D.Conn. 1978)(information stolen from a DEA computer data base)

[89] *E.g., United States v. Genovese*, 409 F.Supp.2d 253 (S.D.N.Y. 2005)(refusing to dismiss on the bases of overbreadth and vagueness grounds an indictment under section 1832 for downloading Miscro soft source code without authorization).

[90] "(a) Whoever, with intent to convert a trade secret,*, that is related to or included in a product that is produced for or placed in interstate or foreign commerce, to the economic benefit of anyone other than the owner thereof, and intending or knowing that the offense will, injure any owner of that trade secret, knowingly – (1) steals, or without authorization appropriates, takes, carries away, or conceals, or by fraud, artifice, or deception obtains such information; (2) without authorization copies, duplicates, sketches, draws photographs, downloads, uploads, alters, destroys, photocopies, replicates, transmits, delivers, sends, mails, communicates, or conveys such information; (3) receives, buys, or possesses such information, knowing the same to have been stolen or appropriated, obtained, or converted without authorization; (4) attempts to commit any offense described in paragraphs (1) through (3); or (5) conspires with one or more other persons to commit any offense described in paragraphs (1) through (3), and one or more of such persons do any act to effect the object of the conspiracy, – shall, except as provided in subsection (b), be fined under this title or imprisoned not more than 10 years, or both.

"(b) Any organization that commits any offense described in subsection (a) shall be fined not more than $5,000,000," 18 U.S.C. 1832.

* "'[T]rade secret' means all forms and types of financial, business, scientific, technical, economic, or engineering information, including patterns, plans, compilations, program devices, formulas, designs, prototypes, methods, techniques, processes, procedures, programs, or codes, whether tangible or intangible, and whether or how stored, compiled, or

memorialized physically, electronically, graphically, photographically, or in writing if –
the owner thereof has taken reasonable measures to keep such information secret; and
the information derives independent economic value, actual or potential, from not being generally known to, and not being readily ascertainable through proper means by, the public," 18 U.S.C. 1 839(3); see generally, *Twenty-Second Survey of White Collar Crime, Intellectual Property Crimes*, 44 AMERICAN CRIMINAL LAW REVIEW 693 (2007); Pooley, Lemley & Toren, *Understanding the Economic Espionage Act of 1996*, 5 TEXAS INTELLECTUAL PROPERTY LAW JOURNAL 177 (1997).

[91] 18 U.S.C. 23 19(b)("(b) Any person who commits an offense under section 506(a)(1)(A) of title 17– (1) shall be imprisoned not more than 5 years, or fined in the amount set forth in this title, or both, if the offense consists of the reproduction or distribution, including by electronic means, during any 1 80-day period, of at least 10 copies or phonorecords, of 1 or more copyrighted works, which have a total retail value of more than $2,500; (2) shall be imprisoned not more than 10 years, or fined in the amount set forth in this title, or both, if the offense is a second or subsequent offense under paragraph (1); and (3) shall be imprisoned not more than 1 year, or fined in the amount set forth in this title, or both, in any other case").

[92] 18 U.S.C. 23 19(c)("Any person who commits an offense under section 506(a)(1)(B) of title 17– (1) shall be imprisoned not more than 3 years, or fined in the amount set forth in this title, or both, if the offense consists of the reproduction or distribution of 10 or more copies or phonorecords of 1 or more copyrighted works, which have a total retail value of $2,500 or more; (2) shall be imprisoned not more than 6 years, or fined in the amount set forth in this title, or both, if the offense is a second or subsequent offense under paragraph (1); and (3) shall be imprisoned not more than 1 year, or fined in the amount set forth in this title, or both, if the offense consists of the reproduction or distribution of 1 or more copies or phonorecords of 1 or more copyrighted works, which have a total retail value of more than $1,000").

[93] 18 U.S.C. 23 19(d)("(d) Any person who commits an offense under section 506(a)(1)(C) of title 17– (1) shall be imprisoned not more than 3 years, fined under this title, or both; (2) shall be imprisoned not more than 5 years, fined under this title, or both, if the offense was committed for purposes of commercial advantage or private financial gain; (3) shall be imprisoned not more than 6 years, fined under this title, or both, if the offense is a second or

subsequent offense; and (4) shall be imprisoned not more than 10 years, fined under this title, or both, if the offense is a second or subsequent offense under paragraph (2)").

[94] 18 U.S.C. 3571.

[95] See generally, *Twenty-Second Survey of White Collar Crime: Money Laundering*, 44 AMERICAN CRIMINAL LAW REVIEW 769 (2007); *Money Laundering: an Overview of 18 U.S. C. 1956 and Related Federal Criminal Law*, RL333 15.

[96] 18 U.S.C. 1956 (text appended).

[97] 18 U.S.C. 1957.

[98] 18 U.S.C. 1956(c)(7)(D), 1957(f)(3).

[99] "The term 'damage' means any impairment to the integrity or availability of data, a program, a system, or information. . . the term 'loss' means an reasonable cost to any victim, including the cost of responding to an offense, conducting a damage assessment, and restoring the data, program, system, or information to its condition prior to the offense, and any revenue lost, cost incurred, or other consequential damages incurred because of interruption of service," 18 U.S.C. 1030(e)(8), (11).

[100] "As used in this section . . . (2) the term 'protected computer' means a computer - (A) exclusively for the use of a financial institution or the United States Government, or, in the case of a computer not exclusively for such use, used by or for a financial institution or the United States Government and the conduct constituting the offense affects that use by or for the financial institution or the Government; or (B) which is used in interstate or foreign commerce or communication including a computer located outside the United States that is used in a manner that affects interstate or foreign commerce or communication of the United States," 18 U.S.C. 1030(e)(2).

[101] *United States v. Lloyd*, 269 F.3d 228, 231 (3d Cir. 2001) involved a former employee charged with triggering a "time bomb" which purged the design and production computer files of the company that fired him. See also, *United States v. Mitra*, 405 F.3d 492 (7th Cir. 2005)(where defendant was found guilty of violating 1030(a)(5) after he disrupted police department's computer-based radio system and thus created public safety problems because the officers could no longer communicate with each other)

[102] Even under an earlier version of the paragraph 1030(a)(5) that outlawed "intentional access . . . without authorization, and by means of . . . such conduct . . . prevent[ing] authorized use of any such computer . . . and thereby causes loss to one or more others of a value aggregating $1,000 or more . . .," the government was not required to show that the defendant

intentionally prevented use nor that he intentionally caused damage "aggregating $1,000 or more"; a demonstration that he intentionally accessed a protected computer without authorization was sufficient, *United States v. Morris*, 928 F.2d 504 (2d Cir. 1991)(Morris, a computer graduate student, was convicted under 18 U.S.C. 1030(a)(5) for releasing a "worm" on the Internet that "spread and multiplied, eventually causing computers at various educational institution and military sites to crash or cease functioning," 928 F.2d at 505); *United States v. Sablan*, 92 F.3d 865, 868 (9th Cir. 1996). Sablan, a disgruntled former bank employee, surreptitiously entered the bank after hours and "called up" and damaged several files from the bank's mainframe on the computer to which she had been assigned prior to her discharge.

[103] *ViChip v. Lee*, 438 F.Supp.2d 1087, 1100 (N.D. Cal. 2006).

[104] *DoJ Computer Crimes*, at 32 ("section 1030(a)(5)(A)(i) requires proof only of the knowing transmission of something to damage a computer without authorization. The government does not need to prove 'access.' Because it is possible to damage a computer without 'accessing' it, this element is easier to prove (except for the mental state requirement). For example, most worms and trojans spread through self-replication, without personally accessing the affected systems").

[105] *See e.g., United States v. Mitra*, 405 F.3d 492, 494-95 (7th Cir. 2005)(paragraph 1030(a) (5) covers jamming a city's computer-operated radio traffic communications system).

[106] S.Rept. 104-357 at 10 (1996)(This would penalize "anyone who knowingly causes the transmission of a program, information, code, or command and intentionally causes damage to a protected computer. This would cover anyone who intentionally damages a computer, regardless of whether they were an outsider or an insider otherwise authorized to access the computer")

[107] *International Airport Centers, L.L.C. v. Citrin*, 440 F.3d 418, 421 (7th Cir. 2006)("Citrin points out that his employment contract authorized him to 'return or *destroy*' data in the laptop when he ceased being employed. But it is unlikely to say the least, that the provision was intended to authorize him to destroy data that he knew the company had no duplicates of and would have wanted to have. . .").

[108] *United States v. Shea*, 493 F.3d 1110, 1115 (9th Cir. 2007).

[109] E.g., 18 U.S.C. 1030(a)(4)(emphasis added)("Whoever . . .(4) knowingly and with intent to defraud, accesses a protected computer *without authorization, or exceeds authorized access . . .*")

[110] S.Rept. 104-357, at 11 (1996)("In sum, under the bill insiders, who are authorized to access a computer, face criminal liability only if they intend to cause damage to a computer, not for recklessly or negligently causing damage. By contrast, outside hackers who break into a computer could be punished for any intentional, reckless, or other damage they cause by their trespass"), quoted in, *United States v. Phillips*, 477 F.3d 215, 219 (5th Cir. 2007); *DoJ Computer Crimes*, at 33 ("Subsections 1030(a)(5)(A)(ii) and (iii) require proof that the defendant intentionally accessed a protected computer without authorization. These subsections do not include the phrase 'exceeds authorized access.' Thus, these subsections do not apply to authorized users of a computer who exceed their authorization (insiders)").

[111] 18 U.S.C. 1030(e)(8). Impairment of the integrity of data or information includes disclosure of confidential information secured through unauthorized access, *Therapeutic Research Facilty v. NBTY, Inc.*, 488 F.Supp.2d 991, 996 (E.D. Cal. 2007); *Shurgard Storage Centers, Inc. v. Safeguard Self Storage, Inc.*, 119 F.Supp.2d 1121, 1 126 (W.D. Wash. 2000)

[112] More precisely, "(B) by conduct described in clause (i), (ii), or (iii) of subparagraph (A), caused (or, in the case of an attempted offense, would, if completed, have caused)– (i) loss to 1 or more persons during any 1-year period (and, for purposes of an investigation, prosecution, or other proceeding brought by the United States only, loss resulting from a related course of conduct affecting 1 or more other protected computers) aggregating at least $5,000 in value," 18 U.S.C. 1030(a)(5)(B)(i).

[113] See S.Rept. 104-357 at 13-4 (1996) (simply paraphrasing the language of the definition).

[114] *United States v. Millot*, 433 F.3d 1057, 1060-6 1 (8th Cir. 2006).

[115] Compare "causes loss or damage to one or more other persons of value aggregating $1,000 or more during any 1-year period," 18 U.S.C. 1030(a)(5)(A)(ii)(II)(aa)(1994 ed.) (emphasis added), with "causes loss aggregating at least $5,000 in value during any 1-year period to one of more individuals," 18 U.S.C. 1030(e)(8)(A)(2000 ed.)(emphasis added).

[116] The argument was made but rejected in United States v. Middleton, 231 F.3d 1207, 1210 (9th Cir. 2000).

[117] S.Rept. 99-432 at 2-3 (1986). The medical records offense had always been tied to the use of interstate computers; 1996 amendments also permit prosecution when the medical records tampering involves one of the other four jurisdictional moorings (i.e., the involvement of federal computers or the computers of financial institutes, or adversely affecting the use of computers by the government or financial institutions).

[118] *United States v. Trotter*, 478 F.3d 918, 921, 922 (8th Cir. 2007); *United States v. Sutcliffe*, 505 F.3d 944, 953 (9th Cir. 2007); *United States v. Mitra*, 405 F.3d 492, 496 (7th Cir. 2005).

[119] "As used in this section . . . (9) the term 'government entity' includes the Government of the United States, any State or political subdivision of the United States, any foreign country, and any state, province, municipality, or other political subdivision of a foreign country," 18 U.S.C. 1030(e)(9)

[120] "Whoever . . . intentionally, without authorization to access any nonpublic computer of a *department or agency of the United States*, accesses such a computer of *that department or agency that is exclusively for the use of the Government of the United States* or, in the case of a computer not exclusively for such use, is used by or for the Government of the United States and such conduct affects that use by or for the Government of the United States. . . ." 18 U.S.C. 1030(a)(3)(emphasis added).

[121] "(e) As used in this section . . . (7) the term 'department of the United States' means the legislative or judicial branch of the Government or one of the executive departments enumerated in section 101 of title 5," 18 U.S.C. 1030(e)(7).

[122] "As used in this title: The term 'department' means one of the executive departments enumerated in section 1 [now section 1010] of Title 5, unless the context shows that such term was intended to describe the executive, legislative, or judicial branches of the government. The term 'agency' includes any department, independent establishment, commission, administration, authority, board or bureau of the United States or any corporation in which the United States has a proprietary interest, unless the context shows that such term was intended to be used in a more limited sense," 18 U.S.C. 6.

[123] "(e) As used in this section. . . (4) the term financial institution' means – (A) an institution with deposits insured by the Federal Deposit Insurance Corporation; (B) the Federal Reserve or a member of the Federal Reserve including any Federal Reserve Bank; (C) a credit union with accounts insured by the National Credit Union Administration; (D) a member of the Federal home loan bank system and any home loan bank; (E) any institution of the Farm Credit System under the Farm Credit Act of 1971; (F) a broker-dealer registered with the Securities and Exchange Commission pursuant to section 15 of the Securities Exchange Act of 1934; (G) the Securities Investor Protection Corporation; (H) a branch or agency of a foreign bank (as such terms are defined in paragraphs (1) and (3) of section 1(b) of the International Banking Act of 1978); (I) an organization operating under

section 25 or section 25(a) of the Federal Reserve Act," 18 U.S.C. 1030(e)(4).

[124] "As used in this title, the term 'financial institution' means – (1) an insured depository institution (as defined in section 3(c)(2) of the Federal Deposit Insurance Act); (2) a credit union with accounts insured by the National Credit Union Share Insurance Fund; (3) a Federal home loan bank or a member, as defined in section 2 of the Federal Home Loan Bank Act (12 U.S.C. 1422), of the Federal home loan bank system; (4) a System institution of the Farm Credit System, as defined in section 5.35(3) of the Farm Credit Act of 1971; (5) a small business investment company, as defined in section 103 of the Small Business Investment Act of 1958 (15 U.S.C. 662); (6) a depository institution holding company (as defined in section 3(w)(1) of the Federal Deposit Insurance Act; (7) a Federal Reserve bank or a member bank of the Federal Reserve System; (8) an organization operating under section 25 or section 25(a) of the Federal Reserve Act; or (9) a branch or agency of a foreign bank (as such terms are defined in paragraphs (1) and (3) of section 1(b) of the International Banking Act of 1978)," 18 U.S.C. 20.

[125] Section 805(c) of the Antiterrorism and Effective Death Penalty Act of 1996, 110 Stat. 1305, instructed the United States Sentencing Commission to adjust the applicable sentencing guidelines so that any violation of paragraph 1030(a)(5) would be punishable by imprisonment for not less than six months. The Commission did so with respect to any violations occurring on or after November 1, 1997, U.S.S.G. §2b 1.3(d), 62 *Fed.Reg.* 26620- 621 (May 14, 1997). Section 814(f) of the USA PATRIOT Act, 28 U.S.C. 994 note, instructed the Commission to amend the Guidelines to ensure the imposition of appropriate penalties "without regard to any mandatory minimum term of imprisonment." For a criticism of these increased penalties, see Skibell, *Cybercrimes & Misdemeanors: A Reevaluation of the Computer Fraud and Abuse Act*, 18 BERKELEY TECHNOLOGY LAW JOURNAL 909, 934 (2003).

[126] The Homeland Security Act added this provision; the USA PATRIOT Act increased the penalty for second or subsequent offenses from imprisonment for not more than 10 to imprisonment for not more than 20 years, and the penalty for intentionally causing damage to a protected computer through a knowing transmission from imprisonment for not more than five years to imprisonment for not more than 10 years. The applicable Sentencing Guideline sets the sentencing ranges for paragraph 1030(a)(5) violations

according to the amount of damage done, the number of victims, and any risk of death or serious injury, U.S.S.G. §2B1.1.

[127] 18 U.S.C. 5032.

[128] See e.g., *United States v. O'Brien*, 435 F.3d 36, 41 (1st Cir. 2006)("The district judge calculated the guideline range . . . adding 6 levels for a loss of $25,000-$40,000, U.S.S.G. §2B1.1, and then adding 2 levels for obstruction of justice, U.S.S.G. §3C1.1, and 2 levels for use of a special skill, U.S.S.G. §3B1 .3"). The court noted that the special skill finding was warranted given the defendant's proficiency in the victimized software which permitted him to instruct others on its use, *id.*

[129] "(Apply the greatest) If the defendant was convicted of an offense under . . .(ii) 18 U.S.C. 1030(a)(5)(A)(i)[intentionally damaging a protected computer], increase by 4 levels. (iii) 18 U.S.C. 1030, and the offense caused a substantial disruption of a critical infrastructure, increase by 6 levels," U.S.S.G. §2B1 .1(b)(14)(A)(ii), (iii).

[130] "(Apply the greatest) If the offense – (A) (i) involved 10 or more victims. . . increase by 2 levels; (B) involved 50 or more victims, increase by 4 levels; or (C) involved 250 or more victims, increase by 6 levels," U.S.S.G. §2B1.1(b)(2).

[131] U.S.S.G. §2B 1.1 (b)(1). Accompanying Application Note (3)(A)(iii) provides, "Offenses Under 18 U.S.C. §1030. – In the case of an offense under 18 U.S.C. § 1030, actual loss includes the following pecuniary harm, regardless of whether such pecuniary harm was reasonably foreseeable: any reasonable cost to any victim, including the cost of responding to an offense, conducting a damage assessment, and restoring the data, program, system, or information to its condition prior to the offense, and any revenue lost, cost incurred, or other damages incurred because of interruption of service."

[132] 18 U.S.C. 981(a)(1)(C), 982(a)(2)(B).

[133] 18 U.S.C. 3663A(c)(1)(A)(ii)

[134] E.g., *United States v. Shea*, 493 F.3d 1110, 1114 (9th Cir. 2007); *United States v. Perry*, 479 F.3d 885, 888 (D.C. Cir. 2007); *United States v. Phillips*, 477 F.3d 215, 217 (5th Cir. 2007); *United States v. Schuster*, 467 F.3d 614, 616 (7th Cir. 2006); *United States v. Millot*, 433 F.3d 1057, 1060 (8th Cir. 2006).

[135] "(g) Any person who suffers damage or loss by reason of a violation of this section may maintain a civil action against the violator to obtain compensatory damages and injunctive relief or other equitable relief. A civil action for a violation of this section may be brought only if the conduct involves 1 of the factors set forth in clause (i), (ii), (iii), (iv), or (v) of

subsection (a)(5)(B). Damages for a violation involving only conduct described in subsection (a)(5)(B)(i) are limited to economic damages. No action may be brought under this subsection unless such action is begun within 2 years of the date of the act complained of or the date of the discovery of the damage. No action may be brought under this subsection for the negligent design or manufacture of computer hardware, computer software, or firmware," 18 U.S.C. 1030(g).

The damages described in clauses (a)(5)(B)(i) through (v) are: "(i) loss to 1 or more persons during any 1-year period (and, for purposes of an investigation, prosecution, or other proceeding brought by the United States only, loss resulting from a related course of conduct affecting 1 or more other protected computers) aggregating at least $5,000 in value; (ii) the modification or impairment, or potential modification or impairment, of the medical examination, diagnosis, treatment, or care of 1 or more individuals; (iii) physical injury to any person; (iv) a threat to public health or safety; or (v) damage affecting a computer system used by or for a government entity in furtherance of the administration of justice, national defense, or national security." See, *America Online, Inc. v. National Health Care Discount, Inc.*, 174 F.Supp.2d 890, 899 (N.D. Iowa 2001)(sending bulk unauthorized and unsolicited e-mail to the Internet service provider's customers violated paragraph 1030(a)(2)).

Although subsection 1030(g) applies to any violation under any of the paragraphs of section 1030, it is discussed at greater length below in connection with paragraph 1030(a)(5)(relating to inflicting damage upon a computer).

[136] "Any person who suffers damage or loss by reason of a violation of this section may maintain a civil action against the violator to obtain compensatory damages and injunctive relief or other equitable relief. A civil action for a violation of this section may be brought only if the conduct involves 1 of the factors set forth in clause (i), (ii), (iii), (iv), or (v) of subsection (a)(5)(B). Damages for a violation involving only conduct described in subsection (a)(5)(B)(i) are limited to economic damages. No action may be brought under this subsection unless such action is begun within two years of the date of the act complained of or the date of the discovery of the damage. No action may be brought under this subsection for the negligent design or manufacture of computer hardware, computer software, or firmware,"18 U.S.C. 1030(g).

The damages described in clauses 1030(a)(5)(B)(i) through (v) are: "(i) loss to 1 or more persons during any 1-year period (and, for purposes of an investigation, prosecution or other proceeding brought by the United States only, loss resulting from a related course of conduct affecting 1 or more other protected computers) aggregating at least $5,000 in value; (ii) the modification or impairment, or potential modification or impairment, of the medical examination, diagnosis, treatment, or care of 1 or more individuals; (iii) physical injury to any person; (iv) a threat to public health or safety; or (v) damage affecting a computer system used by or for a government entity in furtherance of the administration of justice, national defense, or national security." Under section 1030(g) the plaintiffs must show actual "quantifiable" damage. See e.g., *Pearl Investments v. Standard I/O*, 257 F.Supp.2d 326, 349 (D.Me. 2003) (slowing of system's speed and operation did not meet monetary threshold for civil action under 1030(g)).

[137] Black's defines compensatory damages as those damages "sufficient in amount to indemnify the injured person for the loss suffered," BLACK'S LAW DICTIONARY, *Damages* (8th ed. 2004). It recognizes no separate definition for "economic damages," but the term is defined elsewhere in Title 18 of the United States Code as "the replacement costs of lost or damaged property or records, the cost of repeating an interrupted or invalidated experiment, or the loss of profits," 18 U.S.C. 43(d)(3).

[138] Who can be a victim has also been broadly defined by the courts, and rights to civil remedies under the statute have been extended to third parties. The court in *Theofel v. Farey-Jones*, 359 F.3d 1066, 1078 (9th Cir. 2004), emphasized that the statute extends a civil remedy to *any* person who suffers loss or damage, thus "[i]ndividuals other than the computer's owner may be proximately harmed by unauthorized access, particularly if they have rights to data stored on it."

[139] "Whoever . . . (7) with intent to extort from any *person, firm, association, educational institution, financial institution, government entity, or other legal entity*, any money or other thing of value . . ." 18 U.S.C. 1030(a)(7)(emphasis added)(the 2002 amendments struck out "firm, association, educational institution, financial institution, government entity, or other legal entity")

[140] For some of the difficulties associated with possible manufacturer liability under subsection 1030(g) prior to amendment see, *In re America Online, Inc.*, 168 F.Supp.2d 1359 (S.D.Fla. 2001)(allegations that provider's software damaged customers' computers); *Thurmond v. Compaq Computer Corp.*, 171 F.Supp.2d 667 (E.D. Tex. 2001)(floppy disk controllers that allegedly corrupted or destroyed data); *Hayes v. Packard Bell NEC, Inc.*, 193 F.Supp.2d 910 (E.D.Tex. 2001)(same); *Christian v. Sony Corp. of America*, 152 F.Supp.2d 1184 (D.Minn. 200 1)(same).

[141] The USA PATRIOT Act enlarged the definition of federal crimes of terrorism, 18 U.S.C. 2332b(g)(5)(B), to include intentionally damaging a protected computer if the offense involves either impairing medical care, causing physical injury, threatening public health or safety, or damaging a governmental justice, national defense, or national security computer system, 18 U.S.C. 2332b(g)(5)(B)(i)("the term 'federal crime of terrorism means' means an offense that . . . (B) is a violation of – (i) section . . . 1030(a)(5)(A)(i) resulting in damage as defined in 1030(a)(5)(B)(ii) through (v) . . . of this title").

[142] 18 U.S.C. 3286(a). A federal crime of terrorism that results in or involves the risk of serious injury can be prosecuted at any time, 18 U.S.C. 3286(b).

[143] 18 U.S.C. 3583. Federal courts generally impose a term of supervised release whenever they sentence an offender to prison for more than one year, id., U.S.S.G. §5D1 .1. Other than for certain drug offenses and sex crimes, the maximum length of a term of supervised release is 5 years, 18 U.S.C. 3583(b). Conditions of supervised release are not unlike those for probation or parole; the offender comes under the supervision of the Probation Service subject court designated restrictions and obligations, 18 U.S.C. 3583(d).

[144] "(b) It shall be unlawful for any person through a pattern of racketeering activity or through collection of an unlawful debt to acquire or maintain, directly or indirectly, any interest in or control of any enterprise which is engaged in, or the activities of which affect, interstate or foreign commerce.

"(c) It shall be unlawful for any person employed by or associated with any enterprise engaged in, or the activities of which affect, interstate or foreign commerce, to conduct or participate, directly or indirectly, in the conduct of such enterprise's affairs through a pattern of racketeering activity or collection of unlawful debt," 18 U.S.C. 1 962(b), (c)

[145] "(f)(1) Whoever maliciously damages or destroys, or attempts to damage or destroy, *by means of fire or an explosive*, any building, vehicle, or other personal or real property in whole or in part owned or possessed by, or leased to, the United States, or any department or agency thereof, shall be imprisoned for not less than 5 years and not more than 20 years, fined under this title, or both. . . . 18 U.S.C. 844(f)(emphasis added).

"Whoever unlawfully cuts, or wantonly injures or destroys any tree growing, standing, or being upon any land of the United States . . . shall be fined under this title or imprisoned not more than one year, or both," 18 U.S.C. 1853.

[146] "(a) Whoever willfully and unlawfully conceals, removes, mutilates, obliterates, or destroys, or attempts to do so, or, with intent to do so takes and carries away any record, proceeding, map, book, paper, document, or other thing, filed or deposited with any clerk or officer of any court of the United States, or in any public office, or with any judicial or public officer of the United States, shall be fined under this title or imprisoned not more than three years, or both.

"(b) Whoever, having the custody of any such record, proceeding, map, book, document, paper, or other thing, willfully and unlawfully conceals, removes, mutilates, obliterates, falsifies, or destroys the same, shall be fined under this title or imprisoned not more than three years, or both; and shall forfeit his office and be disqualified from holding any office under the United States. As used in this subsection, the term "office" does not include the office held by any person as a retired officer of the Armed Forces of the United States," 18 U.S.C. 2071.

[147] MERRIAM WEBSTER'S COLLEGIATE DICTIONARY, 802 (10th ed. 1996).

[148] *United States v. Rosner*, 352 F.Supp. 915, 919 (S.D.N.Y. 1972).

[149] See, e.g., 26 U.S.C. 601 1(e)(1)("The Secretary shall prescribe regulations providing standards for determining which returns must be filed on magnetic media or in other machine-readable form."); IRS Pub. 3112 (2007); 26 C.F.R. §301.7502-1(d) ("Electronically filed documents– (1) In general. A document filed electronically with an electronic return transmitter. . . in the manner and time prescribed by the Commissioner is deemed to be filed on the date of the electronic postmark . . .given by the authorized electronic return transmitter. Thus, if the electronic postmark is timely, the document is considered filed timely although it is received by the agency, officer, or office after the last date, or the last day of the period, prescribed for filing such document.")

[150] *United States v. Lang*, 364 F.3d 1210 (10th Cir. 2004)(copy of officially filed court document), rem'd for reconsideration in light of *United States v. Booker*, 543 U.S. 220 (2005), reinstated in part, 405 F.3d 1060 (10th Cir. 2005);*United States v. Poindexter*, 725 F.Supp. 13, 19 (D.D.C. 1989)(National Security Council records); *Coplon v. United States*, 191 F.2d 749 (D.C.Cir. 1951)(FBI counter-intelligence reports).

[151] "Whoever willfully injures or commits any depredation against any property of the United States, or of any department or agency thereof, or any property which has been or is being manufactured or constructed for the

United States, or any department or agency thereof, or attempts to commit any of the foregoing offenses, shall be punished as follows:

"If the damage or attempted damage to such property exceeds the sum of $1,000, by a fine under this title or imprisonment for not more than ten years, or both; if the damage or attempted damage to such property does not exceed the sum of $1,000, by a fine under this title or by imprisonment for not more than one year, or both." 18 U.S.C. 1361.

[152] *United States v. Urfer* 287 F.3d 663, 666 (7th Cir. 2002); but see, *United States v. Bangert*, 645 F.2d 1297, 1305 (8th Cir. 1981).

[153] *United States v. Komisaruk*, 885 F.2d 490 (9th Cir. 1989).

[154] *United States v. Morris*, 928 F.2d 504 (2d Cir. 1991).

[155] 18 U.S.C. 1362; 18 U.S.C. 3571. Section 1362 provides in full that: "Whoever willfully or maliciously injures or destroys any of the works, property, or material of any radio, telegraph, telephone or cable, line, station, or system, or other means of communication, operated or controlled by the United States, or used or intended to be used for military or civil defense functions of the United States, whether constructed or in process of construction, or willfully or maliciously interferes in any way with the working or use of any such line, or system, or willfully or maliciously obstructs, hinders, or delays the transmission of any communication over any such line, or system, or attempts or conspires to do such an act, shall be fined under this title or imprisoned not more than ten years, or both

"In the case of any works, property, or material, not operated or controlled by the United States, this section shall not apply to any lawful strike activity, or other lawful concerted activities for the purposes of collective bargaining or other mutual aid and protection which do not injure or destroy any line or system used or intended to be used for the military or civil defense functions of the United States."

[156] *United States v. Sablan*, 92 F.3d 865, 867-69 (9th Cir. 1996). As originally worded, the paragraph penalized anyone who "intentionally accesse[d] a Federal interstate computer . . . and by means of . . . such conduct . . . damage[d] . . . information in such . . . computer," 18 U.S.C. 1030(a)(5)(1988 ed.). Defendants in *Morris* and *Sablan* argued unsuccessfully that the government was required to show that offender had both intentionally accessed a federal computer *and* had intentionally damaged information in the computer. The current wording eliminates the grounds for such contentions.

[157] Violations, attempted violations, and conspiracies to violate the provisions of section 32 are all punishable by imprisonment for not more than 20 years

and/or a fine of not more than $250,000, 18 U.S.C. 32(a); 18 U.S.C. 3571; violations that result in death are punishable by life imprisonment or death, 18 U.S.C. 34. Section 32 reads in pertinent part: "(a) Whoever willfully – (1) sets fire to, damages, destroys, disables, or wrecks any aircraft in the special aircraft jurisdiction of the United States or any civil aircraft used, operated, or employed in interstate, overseas, or foreign air commerce; (2) places or causes to be placed a destructive device or substance in, upon, or in proximity to, or otherwise makes or causes to be made unworkable or unusable or hazardous to work or use, any such aircraft, or any part or other materials used or intended to be used in connection with the operation of such aircraft, if such placing or causing to be placed or such making or causing to be made is likely to endanger the safety of any such aircraft; (3) sets fire to, damages, destroys, or disables any air navigation facility, or interferes by force or violence with the operation of such facility, if such fire, damaging, destroying, disabling, or interfering is likely to endanger the safety of any such aircraft in flight; (4) with the intent to damage, destroy, or disable any such aircraft, sets fire to, damages, destroys, or disables or places a destructive device or substance in, upon, or in proximity to, any appliance or structure, ramp, landing area, property, machine, or apparatus, or any facility or other material used, or intended to be used, in connection with the operation, maintenance, loading, unloading or storage of any such aircraft or any cargo carried or intended to be carried on any such aircraft; (5) interferes or disables, with intent to endanger the safety of any person or with a reckless disregard for the safety of human life, anyone engaged in the authorized operation of such aircraft or any air navigation facility aiding in the navigation of any such aircraft; (6)performs an act of violence against or incapacitates any individual on any such aircraft, if such act of violence or incapacitation is likely to endanger the safety of such aircraft; (7) communicates information, knowing the information to be false and under circumstances in which such information may reasonably be believed, thereby endangering the safety of any such aircraft in flight; or (8) attempts or conspires to do anything prohibited under paragraphs (1) through (7) of this subsection; shall be fined under this title or imprisoned not more than twenty years or both.

Whoever willfully – . . .(2) destroys a civil aircraft registered in a country other than the United States while such aircraft is in service or causes damage to such an aircraft which renders that aircraft incapable of flight or which is likely to endanger that aircraft's safety in flight; . . . or (4) attempts or conspires to commit an offense described in paragraphs (1) through (3) of this subsection;

shall be fined under this title or imprisoned not more than twenty years, or both. There is jurisdiction over an offense under this subsection if a national of the United States was on board, or would have been on board, the aircraft; an offender is a national of the United States; or an offender is afterwards found in the United States. . . .

Whoever willfully imparts or conveys any threat to do an act which would violate any of paragraphs (1) through (5) of subsection (a) or any of paragraphs (1) through (3) of subsection (b) of this section, with an apparent determination and will to carry the threat into execution shall be fined under this title or imprisoned not more than five years, or both."

[158] 18 U.S.C. 2280; 18 U.S.C. 3571. Section 2280 provides in pertinent part: "(a)(1) In general.– A person who unlawfully and intentionally . . . (C) destroys a ship or causes damage to a ship or to its cargo which is likely to endanger the safe navigation of that ship; (D) places or causes to be placed on a ship, by any means whatsoever, a device or substance which is likely to destroy that ship, or cause damage to that ship or its cargo which endangers or is likely to endanger the safe navigation of that ship; (E) destroys or seriously damages maritime navigational facilities or seriously interferes with their operation, if such act is likely to endanger the safe navigation of a ship; (F) communicates information, knowing the information to be false and under circumstances in which such information may reasonably be believed, thereby endangering the safe navigation of a ship; (G) injures or kills any person in connection with the commission or the attempted commission of any of the offenses set forth in subparagraphs (A) through (F); or (H) attempts or conspires to do any act prohibited under subparagraphs (A) through (G),

shall be fined under this title, imprisoned not more than 20 years, or both; and if the death of any person results from conduct prohibited by this paragraph, shall be punished by death or imprisoned for any term of years or for life.

"(2) Threat to navigation. – A person who threatens to do any act prohibited under paragraph (1) (B), (C) or (E), with apparent determination and will to carry the threat into execution, if the threatened act is likely to endanger the safe navigation of the ship in question, shall be fined under this title, imprisoned not more than 5 years, or both.

"(b) Jurisdiction.–There is jurisdiction over the activity prohibited in subsection (a) – (1) in the case of a covered ship, if – (A) such activity is

committed – (i) against or on board a ship flying the flag of the United States at the time the prohibited activity is committed; (ii) in the United States; or (iii) by a national of the United States or by a stateless person whose habitual residence is in the United States; (B) during the commission of such activity, a national of the United States is seized, threatened, injured or killed; or (C) the offender is later found in the United States after such activity is committed;
in the case of a ship navigating or scheduled to navigate solely within the territorial sea or internal waters of a country other than the United States, if the offender is later found in the United States after such activity is committed; and in the case of any vessel, if such activity is committed in an attempt to compel the United States to do or abstain from doing any act. . . .
"(e) Definitions.– In this section – 'covered ship' means a ship that is navigating or is scheduled to navigate into, through or from waters beyond the outer limit of the territorial sea of a single country or a lateral limit of that country's territorial sea with an adjacent country; 'national of the United States' has the meaning stated in section 101(a)(22) of the Immigration and Nationality Act (8 U.S.C. 1101 (a)(22)); 'territorial sea of the United States' means all waters extending seaward to 12 nautical miles from the baselines of the United States determined in accordance with international law; 'ship' means a vessel of any type whatsoever not permanently attached to the sea-bed, including dynamically supported craft, submersibles or any other floating craft, but does not include a warship, a ship owned or operated by a government when being used as a naval auxiliary or for customs or police purposes, or a ship which has been withdrawn from navigation or laid up; 'United States,' when used in a geographical sense, includes the Commonwealth of Puerto Rico, the Commonwealth of the Northern Mariana Islands and all territories and possessions of the United States."

[159] 18 U.S.C. 1992; 18 U.S.C. 3571.

[160] Violations are punishable by imprisonment for not more than 20 years and/or a fine of not more than $250,000 or, if death results from commission of the offense, by imprisonment for life or death, 18 U.S.C. 33(a); 18 U.S.C. 34; 18 U.S.C. 3571.
Section 18 U.S.C. 33 states in full: "(a) Whoever willfully, with intent to endanger the safety of any person on board or anyone who he believes will board the same, or with a reckless disregard for the safety of human life, damages, disables, destroys, tampers with, or places or causes to be placed any explosive or other destructive substance in, upon, or in proximity to, any motor vehicle which is used, operated, or employed in interstate or

foreign commerce, or its cargo or material used or intended to be used in connection with its operation; or

"Whoever willfully, with like intent, damages, disables, destroys, sets fire to, tampers with, or places or causes to be placed any explosive or other destructive substance in, upon, or in proximity to any garage, terminal, structure, supply, or facility used in the operation of, or in support of the operation of, motor vehicles engaged in interstate or foreign commerce or otherwise makes or causes such property to be made unworkable, unusable, or hazardous to work or use; or

"Whoever, with like intent, willfully disables or incapacitates any driver or person employed in connection with the operation or maintenance of the motor vehicle, or in any way lessens the ability of such person to perform his duties as such; or

"Whoever willfully attempts to do any of the aforesaid acts –

shall be fined under this title or imprisoned not more than twenty years, or both.

"(b) Whoever is convicted of a violation of subsection (a) involving a motor vehicle that, at the time the violation occurred, carried high-level radioactive waste (as that term is defined in section 2(12) of the Nuclear Waste Policy Act of 1982 (42 U.S.C. 1010 1(12))) or spent nuclear fuel (as that term is defined in section 2(23) of the Nuclear Waste Policy Act of 1982 (42 U.S.C. 10101(23))), shall be fined under this title and imprisoned for any term of years not less than 30, or for life.

[161] "(a) Whoever knowingly and willfully damages or attempts to damage the property of an energy facility in an amount that in fact exceeds or would if the attempted offense had been completed have exceeded $100,000, or damages or attempts to damage the property of an energy facility in any amount and causes or attempts to cause a significant interruption or impairment of a function of an energy facility, shall be punishable by a fine under this title or imprisonment for not more than 20 years, or both.

Whoever knowingly and willfully damages or attempts to damage the property of an energy facility in an amount that in fact exceeds or would if the attempted offense had been completed have exceeded $5,000 shall be punishable by a fine under this title, or imprisonment for not more than five years, or both.

For purposes of this section, the term 'energy facility' means a facility that is involved in the production, storage, transmission, or distribution of electricity, fuel, or another form or source of energy, or research, development, or demonstration facilities relating thereto, regardless of

whether such facility is still under construction or is otherwise not functioning, except a facility subject to the jurisdiction, administration, or in the custody of the Nuclear Regulatory Commission or an interstate gas pipeline facility as defined in section 60101 of title 49.
Whoever is convicted of a violation of subsection (a) or (b) that has resulted in the death of any person shall be subject to imprisonment for any term of years or life," 18 U.S.C. 1366.

[162] (a) Whoever, without the authority of the satellite operator, intentionally or maliciously interferes with the authorized operation of a communications or weather satellite or obstructs or hinders any satellite transmission shall be fined in accordance with this title or imprisoned not more than ten years or both," 18 U.S.C. 1367.

[163] See, e.g., ALA.CODE 1975 §§13A-8-102, 13A-8-103; ALASKA STAT. §11.46.740; ARIZ. REV.STAT.ANN. §13-2316; ARK.CODEANN. §5-41-202; CAL.PENAL CODE §502; COLO.REV. STAT.ANN. § 18-5.5-102; CONN.GEN.STAT.ANN. §53a-25 1; DEL.CODEANN. tit. 11 § §934, 936; FLA. STAT.ANN. §§815.04, 815.06; GA.CODEANN. §16-9-93; HAWAII REV.STAT. § §708-892, 708-892.5; IDAHO CODE § 18-2202; ILL.COMP.LAWS ANN. ch.720 ¶5, § § 1 6D-3, 16D-4; IND.CODE ANN. §35-43-1-4; IOWA CODE ANN. §716.6B; KAN.STAT.ANN. §21-3755; KY. REV.STAT.ANN. §§434.845, 434.851; LA.REV.STAT.ANN. §§14:73.2 to 14:73.4, 14:73.7; ME. REV.STAT.ANN. tit.17-A §433; MD.CRIM.CODE ANN. §7-302; MICH.COMP.LAWS ANN. §752.795; MINN. STAT.ANN. §609.88; MISS.CODEANN. §§97-45- 7, 97-45-9; MO.ANN.STAT. §§569.095 to 569.099; MONT.CODE ANN. §45-6-311; NEB.REV.STAT. §28-1345; NEV.REV. STAT. 205.4765; N.H. REV.STAT.ANN. §638: 17;N.J.STAT.ANN. §2C:20-25; N.MEX.STAT. ANN. §30-45-4; N.Y.PENAL LAW §§156.10 to 156.27; N.C.GEN.STAT. §§14-455 to 14-458; N.D. CENT. CODE §12.1-06.1-08; OKLA.STAT.ANN. tit.21 §1953; ORE.REV.STAT. §164.377; PA. STAT. ANN. tit.18 §§ 7612, 7615, 7616; R.I.GEN.LAWS §11-52-4.1; S.C.CODE ANN. §16-16-20; S.D.COD. LAWS §43- 43B-1; TENN.CODE ANN. §39-14-602; TEX.PENAL CODE ANN. §33.02; UTAH CODE ANN. §76-6-703; VT.STAT.ANN. tit.13 §§4105-4105; VA.CODE. §18.2-152.4; WASH.REV.CODE ANN. §§9A.48.070 to 9A.48.100; W.VA.CODE ANN. §61-3C-7; WIS.STAT.ANN. §943.70; WYO.STAT. §§6-3-501 to 6-3-504.

[164] 18 U.S.C. 1961(1), 2332b(g)(5)(B).

[165] "It shall be unlawful for any person employed by or associated with any enterprise engaged in, or the activities of which affect, interstate or foreign

commerce, to conduct or participate, directly or indirectly, in the conduct of such enterprise's affairs through a pattern of racketeering activity or collection of unlawful debt.

"(d) It shall be unlawful for any person to conspire to violate any of the provisions of subsection . . . (c) of this section," 18 U.S.C. 1962(c)(d). See generally, *RICO: A Brief Sketch*, CRS Rept. 96-950.

[166] *P.C. Yonkers, Inc. v. Celebrations the Party and Seasonal Superstore, LLC*, 428 F.3d 504, 508 (3d Cir. 2005)(A claim under CFAA § 1030(a)(4) has four elements: (1) defendant has accessed a 'protected computer;' (2) has done so without authorization or by exceeding such authorization as was granted; (3) has done so 'knowingly' and with 'intent to defraud;' and (4) as a result has 'furthered the intended fraud and obtained anything of value").

[167] H.Rept. 98-894 at 16-7 (1984)("A knowing state of mind with respect to an element of the offense is (1) an awareness of the nature of one' conduct, and (2) an awareness of or a firm belief in the existence of a relevant circumstance such as whether an access device was counterfeit before it was used or trafficked in. The Committee intends that the knowing state of mind requirement may be satisfied by proof that the actor was aware of a high probability of the existence of the circumstances, although a defense should succeed if it is proven that the actor actually believed that the circumstance did not exist after taking reasonable steps to warrant such belief. . .. The Committee intends that the term 'with the intent' have the same culpable state of mind as the term 'purpose' as used in the proposed Model Penal Code (§2.02). The distinction from a knowing state of mind was recently restated by Justice Rehnquist, '. . . a person who causes a particular result is said to act purposefully if he consciously desires that result, whatever the likelihood of that result happening from his conduct, while he is aid to act knowingly if he is aware that result is practically certain to follow from his conduct, whatever his desire may be as to that result.' United States v. Bailey, 444 U.S. 394, 404 (1980)").

[168] S.Rept. 99-432 at 9 (1986)("The Committee was concerned that computer usage that is wholly extraneous to an intended fraud might nevertheless be covered by this subsection if the subsection were patterned directly after the current mail fraud and wire fraud laws. If it were so patterned, the subsection might be construed as covering an individual who had devised a scheme or artifice to defraud solely because used a computer to keep records or to add up his potential 'take' from the crime. The Committee does not believe that a scheme or artifice to defraud should fall under the ambit of subsection (a)(4) merely because the offender signed onto a

computer at some point near to the commission or execution of the fraud. While such a tenuous link might be covered under current law where the instrumentality used is the mails or the wires, the Committee does not consider that link sufficient with respect to computers. To be prosecuted under this subsection, the use of the computer must be more directly linked to the intended fraud. That is, it must be used by the offender without authorization or in excess of his authorization to obtain property of another, which property furthers in the intended fraud").

[169] "The plain language of section 1030(a)(4) emphasizes that more than mere unauthorized use is required: the 'thing obtained' may not merely be the unauthorized use. It is the showing of some additional end – to which the unauthorized access is a means – that is lacking here. The evidence did not show that Czubinski's end was anything more than to satisfy his curiosity by viewing information about friends, acquaintances, and political rivals. No evidence suggests that he printed out, recorded, or sued the information he browsed. No rational jury could conclude beyond a reasonable doubt that Czubinski intended to use or disclose that information, and merely viewing information cannot be deemed the same as obtaining something of value for the purposes of this statute. [The district court, in denying a motion to dismiss the computer fraud counts in the indictment, found that the indictment sufficiently alleged that the confidential taxpayer information was itself a thing of value to Czubinski, given his ends. The indictment, or course, alleged specific uses for the information, such as creating dossiers on KKK members, that were not proven at trial]," United States v. Czubinski, 106 F.3d at 1078 (portions of footnote 15 of the Court's opinion in brackets). See also, United States v. DeMonte, 25 F.3d 343 (6th Cir. 1 994)(authority of sentencing court to order probation instead of imprisonment pursuant to a downward departure, on the basis of extraordinary circumstances, from the applicable sentencing guidelines for a violation of 18 U.S.C. 1030(4) that occurred when the defendant, a Veterans' Administration supervisory accountant made fraudulent entries in a VA computer system that result in payments to a fictitious company).

[170] The governing Sentencing Guideline calculates the applicable sentencing ranges below the statutory 5 and 10 year maximum penalties based on the amount of loss and the number of victims related to the offense, U.S.S.G. §2B1.1.

[171] Civil plaintiffs utilizing 1030(g) tend to have been more likely to successfully litigate under a violation of 1030(a)(4) than in the criminal context. See, e.g., Creative Computing v. Getloaded.com, 386 F.3d 930 (9th

Cir. 2004)(court found that plaintiff successfully demonstrated loss of business as economic damages, and that the evidence supported a damage award and injunctive relief).

[172] "Whoever, having devised or intending to devise any scheme or artifice to defraud, or for obtaining money or property by means of false or fraudulent pretenses, representations, or promises, transmits or causes to be transmitted by means of wire, radio, or television communication in interstate or foreign commerce, any writings, signs, signals, pictures, or sounds for the purpose of executing such scheme or artifice, shall be fined under this title or imprisoned not more than five years, or both. If the violation affects a financial institution, such person shall be fined not more than $1,000,000 or imprisoned not more than 30 years, or both," 18 U.S.C. 1343; see generally, *Twenty-Second Survey of White Collar Crime: Mail and Wire Fraud*, 44 AMERICAN CRIMINAL LAW REVIEW 745 (2007); *Criminal and Civil RICO: Traditional Canons of Statutory Interpretation and the Liberal Construction Clause*, 30 COLUMBIA JOURNAL OF LAW & SOCIAL PROBLEMS 41 (1996); Lynch, *RICO: The Crime of Being a Criminal*, 87 COLUMBIA LAW REVIEW 661 (Pts. I & II), 920 (Pts. III & IV) (1987).

[173] *Carpenter v. United States*, 484 U.S. 19, 26 (1987).

[174] *United States v. Martin*, 228 F.3d 1, 16 (1st Cir. 2000); *United States v. Czubinski*, 106 F.3d 1069, 1073-76 (1st Cir. 1997); *United States v. Wang*, 898 F.Supp. 758, 760 (D.Colo. 1995); *United States v. Seidlitz*, 589 F.2d 152, 160 (4th Cir. 1978)

[175] Olivenbaum, *<CTRL><ALT><DELETE>: Rethinking Federal Computer Crime Legislation*, SETON HALL LAW REVIEW 574, 625 (1997).

[176] Each was enacted in part due to concerns about the breadth of a more narrowly crafted ancestor whose prohibitions continue in effect. In the case of section 1029, there were questions whether 15 U.S.C. 1 644 (Truth in Lending Act) that outlaws the fraudulent use of credit cards could reach counterfeiting or the use of stolen credit card account numbers, H.Rept. 894, 98th Cong., 2d Sess. 5 (1984). In the case of section 1030, similar questions were raised about sweep of 15 U.S.C. 1 693n (Electronic Funds Transfer Act) that outlaws the fraudulent use of bank debit cards), Id. See generally, *What Constitutes Violation of 18 USCS §1029, Prohibiting Fraud or Related Activity in Connection with Credit Card or Other Credit Access Device*, 115 ALR FED 213 (2005).

[177] P.L. 98-473, 98 Stat. 2183, 2190 (1984). Section 1029 was amended by P.L. 99-646, 100 Stat. 3601 (1986); P.L. 101-647, 104 Stat. 4831 (1990); P.L. 103-322, 108 Stat. 2087, 2148 (1994); P.L. 103-414, 108 Stat. 4291 (1994); P.L. 104-294, 110 Stat. 3501 (1996); P.L. 105- 172, 112 Stat. 53 (1998); P.L. 107-25,115 Stat. 342 (2001); P.L. 107-273, 116 Stat. 1808 (2002).

[178] The cases suggest that the interstate nexus must be clearly identifiable but have yet to identify the point, if any, at which the connection becomes too tenuous to support a claim of an affect on interstate commerce, see e.g., *United States v. Bolton*, 68 F.3d 396, 400 n.3 (10th Cir. 1 995)(large majority of stolen credit cards in the defendant's possession had out of state addresses printed on them); *United States v. Clayton*, 108 F.3d 1114, 1118 (9th Cir. 1997). Since the misconduct proscribed is commercial in nature the question is not one of Congressional power but whether in a given case the government can and has proven that the particular misconduct "affects interstate or foreign commerce," compare *United States v. Morrison*, 529 U.S. 598, 608-9 (2000) and *United States v. Lopez*, 514 U.S. 549, 558-59 (1 995)(Congress may regulate the instrumentalities and use of the channels of interstate commerce and activities that have a substantial relation to interstate commerce), with, *Jones v. United States*, 529 U.S. 848, 852 (2000) (a statute that outlaws the destruction of property "used" in commerce does not protect residential property not shown to have been used for any commercial purpose) and *Gonzales v. Raich*, 545 U.S. 1, 17 (2005) (federal government may regulate "an economic class" of intrastate activities–even if the activity itself, is noncommercial–if they are rationally related to or substantially effecting interstate commerce).

[179] As discussed below section 1029 also overlaps paragraph 1030(a)(6) that relates to trafficking in a particular access device, computer passwords.

[180] "'With intent to defraud' means that the offender has a conscious objective, desire or purpose to deceive another person, and to induce such other person, in reliance upon such deception, to assume, create, transfer, alter or terminate a right, obligation, or power with reference to property," S.Rept. 368 at 7.

[181] "Whoever – (1) knowingly and with intent to defraud produces, uses, or traffics in one or more counterfeit access devices . . . shall, if the offense affects interstate or foreign commerce, be punished as provided in subsection (c) of this section," 18 U.S.C. 1029(a)(1).

[182] "The term 'fictitious' is intended to cover a number of different types of counterfeit devices, including representations, depictions or facsimiles of an access device. The definition is intended to be sufficiently broad to cover

components of an access device or a counterfeit access device, but would exclude indistinguishable raw materials. The components would include elements of devices that are legitimate but obtained or used with an intent to defraud. Thus, any identifiable component, whether it is in fact an actual component that has been obtained in some fashion by a perpetrator with an intent to defraud or a false or counterfeit substitute for a legitimate component, would fall within the definition of counterfeit access device. The committee intends the term 'component' to include incomplete access devices or counterfeit access devices, such as any mag strips, holograms, signature panels, microchips, and blank cards of so-called 'white plastic.'" H.Rept. 98-894 at 19 (1984).

[183] "Whoever . . . knowingly and with intent to defraud traffics in or uses one or more unauthorized access devices during any one-year period, and by such conduct obtains anything of value aggregating $1,000 or more during that period . . . shall, if the offense affects interstate or foreign commerce, be punished as provided in subsection (c) of this section," 18 U.S.C. 1029(a)(2).

[184] "Whoever . . . knowingly and with intent to defraud effects transactions, with 1 or more access devices issued to another person or persons, to receive payment or any other thing of value during any 1-year period the aggregate value of which is equal to or greater than $1,000 . . . shall, if the offense affects interstate or foreign commerce, be punished as provided in subsection (c) of this section," 18 U.S.C. 1 029(a)(5).

[185] "Whoever . . . knowingly and with intent to defraud possesses fifteen or more devices which are counterfeit or unauthorized access devices . . . shall, if the offense affects interstate or foreign commerce, be punished as provided in subsection (c) of this section," 18 U.S.C. 1029(a)(3).

[186] "Whoever . . . knowingly, and with intent to defraud, produces, traffics in, has control or custody of, or possesses device-making equipment . . . shall, if the offense affects interstate or foreign commerce, be punished as provided in subsection (c) of this section," 18 U.S.C. 1 029(a)(4).

[187] "As used in this section . . . the term 'device-making equipment' means any equipment, mechanism, or impression designed or primarily used for making an access device or a counterfeit access device," 18 U.S.C. 1029(e)(6)

[188] "Whoever . . . without the authorization of the issuer of the access device, knowingly and with intent to defraud solicits a person for the purpose of -- (A) offering an access device; or (B) selling information regarding or an application to obtain an access device . . . shall, if the offense affects

interstate or foreign commerce, be punished as provided in subsection (c) of this section," 18 U.S.C. 1029(a)(6).

[189] "Whoever . . . knowingly and with intent to defraud uses, produces, traffics in, has control or custody of, or possesses a telecommunications instrument that has been modified or altered to obtain unauthorized use of telecommunications services . . . shall, if the offense affects interstate or foreign commerce, be punished as provided in subsection (c) of this section," 18 U.S.C. 1029(a)(7).

[190] "Whoever . . . knowingly and with intent to defraud uses, produces, traffics in, has control or custody of, or possesses a scanning receiver . . . shall, if the offense affects interstate or foreign commerce, be punished as provided in subsection (c) of this section," 18 U.S.C. 1029(a)(8).

[191] "The term 'scanning receiver' means a device or apparatus that can be used to intercept a wire or electronic communication in violation of chapter 119 or to intercept an electronic serial number, mobile identification number, or other identifier of any telecommunications service, equipment, or instrument," 18 U.S.C. 1029(e)(8).

[192] "Whoever . . . knowingly and with intent to defraud uses, produces, traffics in, has control or custody of, or possesses hardware or software, knowing it has been configured to insert or modify telecommunication identifying information associated with or contained in a telecommunications instrument so that the instrument may be used to obtain telecommunications service without authorization . . . shall, if the offense affects interstate or foreign commerce, be punished as provided in subsection (c) of this section," 18 U.S.C. 1 029(a)(9).

[193] "Whoever . . . without the authorization of the credit card system member* or its agent, knowingly and with intent to defraud causes or arranges for another person to present to the member or its agent, for payment, 1 or more evidences or records of transactions made by an access device; shall, if the offense affects interstate or foreign commerce, be punished as provided in subsection (c) of this section," 18 U.S.C. 1029(a)(10).

* "As used in this section . . . [t]he term 'credit card system member' means a financial institution or other entity that is a member of a credit card system, including an entity, whether affiliated with or identical to the credit card issuer, that is the sole member of a credit card system," 18 U.S.C. 1029(e)(7).

[194] "Whoever attempts to commit an offense under subsection (a) of this section shall be punished as provided in subsection (c) of this section," 18 U.S.C. 1029(b)(1).

[195] "Whoever is a party to a conspiracy of two or more persons to commit an offense under subsection (a) of this section, if any of the parties engages in any conduct in furtherance of such offense, shall be fined an amount not greater than the amount provided as the maximum fine for such offense under subsection (c) of this section or imprisoned not longer than one-half the period provided as the maximum imprisonment for such offense under subsection (c) of this section, or both," 18 U.S.C. 1 029(b)(2).

[196] Offenders are subject to fines and forfeiture as well, "(1) . . .The punishment for an offense under subsection (a) of this section is – (A) in the case of an offense that does not occur after a conviction for another offense under this section – "(i) if the offense is under paragraph (1), (2), (3), (6), (7), or (10) of subsection (a), a fine under this title or imprisonment for not more than 10 years, or both; and (ii) if the offense is under paragraph (4), (5), (8), or (9), of subsection (a), a fine under this title or imprisonment for not more than 15 years, or both;

in the case of an offense that occurs after a conviction for another offense under this section, a fine under this title or imprisonment for not more than 20 years, or both; and

in either case, forfeiture to the United States of any personal property used or intended to be used to commit the offense.

"(2) Forfeiture procedure.–The forfeiture of property under this section, including any seizure and disposition of the property and any related administrative and judicial proceeding, shall be governed by section 413 of the Controlled Substances Act, except for subsection (d) of that section," 18 U.S.C. 1029(c).

[197] ı"If two or more persons conspire . . . to defraud the United States, or any agency thereof in any manner or for any purpose, and one or more of such persons do any act to effect the object of the conspiracy, each shall be fined under this title or imprisoned not more than five years, or both," 18 U.S.C. 371.

[198] *United States v. Goldberg*, 105 F.3d 770, 773 (1st Cir. 1997); *United States v. Clark*, 139 F.3d 485, 488-89 (5th Cir. 1998); *United States v. Gosselin World Wide Moving*, 41 1F.3d 502, 516 (4th Cir. 2005); *United States v. Shellef*, 507 F.3d 82, 104 (2d Cir. 2007).

[199] *Tanner v. United States*, 483 U.S. 107, 128 (1987), citing, *Dennis v. United States*, 384 U.S. 855, 861 (1966); *Hass v. Henkel*, 216 U.S. 462, 479 (1910); *Glasser v. United States*, 315 U.S. 60, 66 (1942); *Hammerschmidt v. United States*, 265 U.S. 182, 188 (1924); *Gosselin World Wide Moving*,

411 F.3 502, 516 (4th Cir.2005); *United States v. McKee*, 506 F.3d 225, 238 (3d Cir. 2007).

[200] *United States v. Ballistrea*, 101 F.3d 827, 832 (2d Cir. 1996)("so long as deceitful or dishonest means are employed to obstruct governmental functions, the impairment need not involve the violation of a separate statute"); *United States v. Khalife*, 106 F.3d 1300, 1303 (6th Cir. 1997); *United States v. Douglas*, 398 F.3d 407, 412 (6th Cir. 2005)("a conviction under section 371 does not require the government to prove a violation of a separate substantive statute").

[201] *United States v. Shellef*, 507 F.3d 82, 107 (2d Cir. 2007); *United States v. Dean*, 55 F.3d 640, 647 (D.C.Cir. 1994); *United States v. Hansen*, 262 F.3d 1217, 1246 (11th Cir. 2001)("To obtain a conviction under 18 U.S.C. § 371, the government must show: (1) the existence of an agreement to achieve an unlawful objective; (2) the defendant's knowing and voluntary participation in the conspiracy; and (3) the commission of an overt act in furtherance of the conspiracy").

[202] "(a) Whoever knowingly executes, or attempts to execute, any scheme or artifice with the intent – (1) to defraud the United States; or (2) to obtain money or property by means of false or fraudulent pretenses, representations, or promises – in any procurement of property or services as a prime contractor with the United States or as a subcontractor or supplier on a contract in which there is a prime contract with the United States, if the value of the contract, subcontract, or any constituent part thereof, for such property or services is $1,000,000 or more shall, subject to the applicability of subsection (c) of this section, be fined not more than $1,000,000, or imprisoned not more than 10 years, or both.

The fine imposed for an offense under this section may exceed the maximum otherwise provided by law, if such fine does not exceed $5,000,000 and – (1) the gross loss to the Government or the gross gain to a defendant is $500,000 or greater; or (2) the offense involves a conscious or reckless risk of serious personal injury.

The maximum fine imposed upon a defendant for a prosecution including a prosecution with multiple counts under this section shall not exceed $10,000,000. . . ." 18 U.S.C. 1031.

[203] "Whoever, in any matter involving a health care benefit program, knowingly and willfully – (1) falsifies, conceals, or covers up by any trick, scheme, or device a material fact; or (2) makes any materially false, fictitious, or fraudulent statements or representations, or makes or uses any materially false writing or document knowing the same to contain any

materially false, fictitious, or fraudulent statement or entry, in connection with the delivery of or payment for health care benefits, items, or services, shall be fined under this title or imprisoned not more than five years, or both," 18 U.S.C. 1035(a).

[204] "Whoever knowingly makes any false statement or report, or willfully overvalues any land, property or security, for the purpose of influencing in any way the action of the Farm Credit Administration, Federal Crop Insurance Corporation or a company the Corporation reinsures, the Secretary of Agriculture acting through the Farmers Home Administration or successor agency, the Rural Development Administration or successor agency, any Farm Credit Bank, production credit association, agricultural credit association, bank for cooperatives, or any division, officer, or employee thereof, or of any regional agricultural credit corporation established pursuant to law, or a Federal land bank, a Federal land bank association, a Federal Reserve bank, a small business investment company, as defined in section 103 of the Small Business Investment Act of 1958 (15 U.S.C. 662), or the Small Business Administration in connection with any provisions of that act, a Federal credit union, an insured State-chartered credit union, any institution the accounts of which are insured by the Federal Deposit Insurance Corporation, the Office of Thrift Supervision, any Federal home loan bank, the Federal Housing Finance Board, the Federal Deposit Insurance Corporation, the Resolution Trust Corporation, the Farm Credit System Insurance Corporation, or the National Credit Union Administration Board, a branch or agency of a foreign bank (as such terms are defined in paragraphs (1) and (3) of section 1(b) of the International Banking Act of 1978), or an organization operating under section 25 or section 25(a) of the Federal Reserve Act, upon any application, advance, discount, purchase, purchase agreement, repurchase agreement, commitment, or loan, or any change or extension of any of the same, by renewal, deferment of action or otherwise, or the acceptance, release, or substitution of security therefor, shall be fined not more than $1,000,000 or imprisoned not more than 30 years, or both. . . ." 18 U.S.C. 1014.

[205] "Whoever, for the purpose of obtaining any loan or advance of credit from any person, partnership, association, or corporation with the intent that such loan or advance of credit shall be offered to or accepted by the Department of Housing and Urban Development for insurance, or for the purpose of obtaining any extension or renewal of any loan, advance of credit, or mortgage insured by such Department, or the acceptance, release, or

substitution of any security on such a loan, advance of credit, or for the purpose of influencing in any way the action of such Department, makes, passes, utters, or publishes any statement, knowing the same to be false, or alters, forges, or counterfeits any instrument, paper, or document, or utters, publishes, or passes as true any instrument, paper, or document, knowing it to have been altered, forged, or counterfeited, or willfully overvalues any security, asset, or income, shall be fined under this title or imprisoned not more than two years, or both," 18 U.S.C. 1010.

"Whoever, with intent to defraud, makes any false entry in any book of the Department of Housing and Urban Development or makes any false report or statement to or for such Department; or whoever receives any compensation, rebate, or reward, with intent to defraud such Department or with intent unlawfully to defeat its purposes; or whoever induces or influences such Department to purchase or acquire any property or to enter into any contract and willfully fails to disclose any interest which he has in such property or in the property to which such contract relates, or any special benefit which he expects to receive as a result of such contract – shall be fined under this title or imprisoned not more than one year, or both," 18 U.S.C. 1012.

[206] "Whoever makes or presents to any person or officer in the civil, military, or naval service of the United States, or to any department or agency thereof, any claim upon or against the United States, or any department or agency thereof, knowing such claim to be false, fictitious, or fraudulent, shall be imprisoned not more than five years and shall be subject to a fine in the amount provided in this title," 18 U.S.C. 287; see generally, *Twenty-Second Survey of White Collar Crime: False Statements and False Claims*, 44 AMERICAN CRIMINAL LAW REVIEW 491 (2007).

[207] "Whoever knowingly executes, or attempts to execute, a scheme or artifice – (1) to defraud a financial institution; or (2) to obtain any of the moneys, funds, credits, assets, securities, or other property owned by, or under the custody or control of, a financial institution, by means of false or fraudulent pretenses, representations, or promises – shall be fined not more than $1,000,000 or imprisoned not more than 30 years, or both," 18 U.S.C. 1344; see generally, *Twenty-Second Survey of White Collar Crime: Financial Institution Fraud*, 44 AMERICAN CRIMINAL LAW REVIEW 555 (2007).

[208] Whoever, being an officer, director, agent or employee of, or connected in any capacity with any Federal Reserve bank, member bank, depository institution holding company, national bank, insured bank, branch or agency of a foreign bank, or organization operating under section 25 or section

25(a) of the Federal Reserve Act [12 U.S.C.A. ss 601 et seq., 611 et seq.], or a receiver of a national bank, insured bank, branch, agency, or organization or any agent or employee of the receiver, or a Federal Reserve Agent, or an agent or employee of a Federal Reserve Agent or of the Board of Governors of the Federal Reserve System, embezzles, abstracts, purloins or willfully misapplies any of the moneys, funds or credits of such bank, branch, agency, or organization or holding company or any moneys, funds, assets or securities intrusted to the custody or care of such bank, branch, agency, or organization, or holding company or to the custody or care of any such agent, officer, director, employee or receiver, shall be fined not more than $1,000,000 or imprisoned not more than 30 years, or both; but if the amount embezzled, abstracted, purloined or misapplied does not exceed $1,000, he shall be fined under this title or imprisoned not more than one year, or both," 18 U.S.C. 656; see also, 18 U.S.C. 657 (theft or embezzlement by officer or employee of lending, credit or insurance institution); 1005 (false entries by bank officers or employees); 1006 (false entries by officers or employees of federal credit institutions); 1007 (false statemetns to influence the Federal Deposit Insurance Corporation)

[209] "The punishment for an offense under subsection (a) is – (1) a fine under this title, imprisonment for not more than 5 years, or both, if – (A) the offense is committed in furtherance of any felony under the laws of the United States or of any State; or (B) the defendant has previously been convicted under this section or section 1030, or under the law of any State for conduct involving the transmission of multiple commercial electronic mail messages or unauthorized access to a computer system;

a fine under this title, imprisonment for not more than 3 years, or both, if – (A) the offense is an offense under subsection (a)(1); (B) the offense is an offense under subsection (a)(4) and involved 20 or more falsified electronic mail or online user account registrations, or 10 or more falsified domain name registrations; (C) the volume of electronic mail messages transmitted in furtherance of the offense exceeded 2,500 during any 24-hour period, 25,000 during any 30-day period, or 250,000 during any 1-year period; (D) the offense caused loss to one or more persons aggregating $5,000 or more in value during any 1-year period; (E) as a result of the offense any individual committing the offense obtained anything of value aggregating $5,000 or more during any 1-year period; or (F) the offense was undertaken by the defendant in concert with three or more other persons with respect to whom the defendant occupied a position of organizer or leader; and a fine under this title or imprisonment for not more than 1 year, or both, in any other case, " 18 U.S.C. 1037(b).

[210] 18 U.S.C. 1956 (text appended).

[211] 18 U.S.C. 1957.

[212] "(4) the term 'financial transaction' means (A) a transaction* which in any way or degree affects interstate or foreign commerce (i) involving the movement of funds by wire or other means or (ii) involving one or more monetary instruments,** or (iii) involving the transfer of title to any real property, vehicle, vessel, or aircraft, or (B) a transaction involving the use of a financial institution which is engaged in, or the activities of which affect, interstate or foreign commerce in any way or degree," 18 U.S.C. 1956(c)(4).

* "The term 'transaction' includes a purchase, sale, loan, pledge, gift, transfer, delivery, or other disposition, and with respect to a financial institution includes a deposit, withdrawal, transfer between accounts, exchange of currency, loan, extension of credit, purchase or sale of any stock, bond, certificate of deposit, or other monetary instrument, use of a safe deposit box, or any other payment, transfer, or delivery by, through, or to a financial institution, by whatever means effected," 18 U.S.C. 1 956(c)(3).

** "The term 'monetary instruments' means (i) coin or currency of the United States or of any other country, travelers' checks, personal checks, bank checks, and money orders, or (ii) investment securities or negotiable instruments, in bearer form or otherwise in such form that title thereto passes upon delivery," 18 U.S.C. 1956(c)(5).

[213] *United States v. Ables*, 167 F.3d 1021, 1029 (6th Cir. 1999); *United States v. Owens*, 167 F.3d 739, 755 (1st Cir. 1999); *United States v. Meshack*, 225 F.3d 556, 572 (5th Cir. 2000); *United States v. Oliveros*, 275 F.3d 1299, 1303 (1 1th Cir. 2001); *United States v. Ramerez*, 313 F. Supp. 2d 276, 279 (S.D.N.Y. 2004) In *United States v. Lopez*, 514 U.S. 549 (1995), the United States Supreme Court held that Gun Free School Zone Act, which purported to make it a federal crime to possess a gun in or near a school, failed to claim or exhibit the nexus to interstate or foreign commerce necessary to constitute the valid exercise of Congress' legislative authority under the Constitution's commerce clause.

[214] *United States v. Williamson*, 339 F.3d 1295, 1302 (1 1th Cir. 2003) (depositing and cashing checks of proceeds of fraud promoted present and future unlawful activities); *United States v. Rivera*, 295 F.3d 461, 469 (5th Cir. 2002)(bank withdrawal of a portion of the proceeds of a fraudulent

scheme to pay a co-conspirator his share constituted "promotion"); see also, *United States v. Febus*, 218 F.3d 784, 790 (7th Cir. 1999) (operator of illegal gambling enterprise "promoted" the venture for money laundering purposes by paying off winning customers and thereby ensuring their continued patronage); *United States v. Meshack*, 225 F.3d 556, 573 (5th Cir. 2000)(defendant's use of drug money to pay the rent on his girlfriend's apartment where drugs were stored and which was used "in an attempt to conceal the conspiracy" was sufficient to establish promotion of the drug trafficking conspiracy); *United States v. Bockius*, 228 F.3d 305, 310 n.8 (3d Cir. 2000)(noting its holding in *United States v. Paramo*, 998 F.2d 1212, 1218 (3d Cir. 1993) (that a rationale jury could have concluded that cashing embezzled IRS checks was intended to promote the antecedent frauds).

[215] *United States v. Sokolow*, 91 F.3d 396, 408 (3d Cir. 1996); *United States v. Rivera- Hernandez*, 497 F3d 71,76 (1st Cir. 2007); *United States v. Rayborn*, 491 F.3d 513, 517 (6th Cir. 2007). Or more precisely, "(a) Whoever, in any of the circumstances set forth in subsection (d), knowingly engages or attempts to engage in a monetary transaction in criminally derived property that is of a value greater than $10,000 and is derived from specified unlawful activity, shall be punished as provided in subsection (b). "(b)(1) Except as provided in paragraph (2), the punishment for an offense under this section is a fine under title 18, United States Code, or imprisonment for not more than ten years or both. (2) The court may impose an alternate fine to that imposable under paragraph (1) of not more than twice the amount of the criminally derived property involved in the transaction.

In a prosecution for an offense under this section, the Government is not required to prove the defendant knew that the offense from which the criminally derived property was derived was specified unlawful activity.

The circumstances referred to in subsection (a) are – (1) that the offense under this section takes place in the United States or in the special maritime and territorial jurisdiction of the United States; or (2) that the offense under this section takes place outside the United States and such special jurisdiction, but the defendant is a United States person (as defined in section 3077 of this title, but excluding the class described in paragraph (2)(D) of such section).." 18 U.S.C. 1957(a)-(d).

[216] "As used in this section – (1) the term 'monetary transaction' means the deposit, withdrawal, transfer, or exchange, in or affecting interstate or foreign commerce, of funds or a monetary instrument (as defined in section

1956(c)(5) of this title) by, through, or to a financial institution (as defined in section 1956 of this title), including any transaction that would be a financial transaction under section 1956(c)(4)(B) of this title, but such term does not include any transaction necessary to preserve a person's right to representation as guaranteed by the sixth amendment to the Constitution," 18 U.S.C. 1 957(f)(1).

[217] United States v. Aramony, 88 F.3d 1369, 1386 (4th Cir. 1996); United States v. Kunzman, 54 F.3d 1522, 1527 (10th Cir. 1995); it is enough, for example, for the government to show that the transaction involved a federally insured bank, *United States v. Benjamin*, 252 F.3d 1, 8 (1st Cir. 2001); *United States v. Ford*, 184 F.3d 566, 583-84 (6th Cir. 1999); *United States v. Wadena*, 152 F.3d 831, 853 (8th Cir. 1998).

[218] ALA.CODE §§13A-8-102, 13A-8-103; ALASKA STAT. §11.46.740; ARIZ.REV. STAT.ANN. §13-2316, 2316.02; ARK.CODE ANN. §5-41-103; CAL.PENAL CODE §502; COLO.REV. STAT.ANN. §18-5.5-102; CONN.GEN.STAT.ANN. §53a-251; DEL.CODEANN. tit.11 §§933; FLA.STAT. ANN. §815.04; GA.CODE ANN. §16-9-93, 93.1; HAWAII REV.STAT. §708-891, 891.5; IDAHO CODE § 18-2202; ILL. COMP.STAT.ANN. 720 5/16D-5; KAN.STAT.ANN. §21- 3755; KY.REV.STAT.ANN. §434.845; LA. REV.STAT.ANN. § 14:73.5; ME. REV.STAT.ANN. tit.17-A §433; MICH.COMP.LAWS ANN. §752.794; MINN.STAT.ANN. §609.89; MISS. CODE ANN. §97-45-3; MONT.CODE ANN. §45-6-311; NEB.REVSTAT. §28-1344; NEV.REV. STAT. 205.4765, 481; N.H.REV.STAT.ANN. §638:17; N.J.STAT.ANN. §2C:20-25; N.MEX.STAT. ANN. §30-45-3; N.Y. PENAL LAW §§156.10 to 156.30; N.C.GEN.STAT. §§14-454, 14-454.1, 14-458; N.D. CENT.CODE § 12.1-06.1-08; OKLA.STAT.ANN. tit.21 § 1953; ORE.REV.STAT. §164.377; PA.STAT.ANN. tit.18 §§7611, 7613; R.I.GEN.LAWS §11-52-2; S.C. CODE ANN. § 16-16-20; S.D.COD.LAWS §43-43B-1; TENN.CODE ANN. §39-14-602; TEX.PENAL CODE ANN. §33.02; UTAH CODE ANN. §76-10-1801; VT.STAT.ANN. tit. 13 §4103; VA.CODE § 18.2- 152.3; WASH. REV.CODE ANN. §9A.52. 110; W.VA.CODE ANN. §61-3C-4; WIS.STAT.ANN. §943.70; WYO.STAT. §6-3-502.

[219] See e.g., *United States v. Kammersell*, 196 F.3d 1137, 1138-140 (10th Cir. 1999)(a threat communicated between two computers in Utah involved interstate communications because the communications was forwarded by way of AOL's server in Virginia).

[220] *United States v. Ivanov*, 175 F.Supp.2d 367, 374 (D.Conn. 2001).

[221] Section 814(d)(1), P.L. 107-56, 115 Stat. 384 (2001), amending 18 U.S.C. 1030j(e)(2)(B).

[222] The circuits are divided over the question of whether in order to convict under some of the threat statutes, the government must show that the defendant intended the victim to feel threatened or merely intended the conduct that a reasonable person would consider threatening. United States v. Darby, 37 F.3d 1059, 1963-66 (4th Cir. 1994)(and the conflicting cases cited there)("to establish a violation of section 87 5(c) the government must establish that the defendant intended to transmit the interstate communication and that the communication contained a true threat. . . . The government does not have to prove that the defendant subjectively intended for the recipient to understand the communication as a threat"); *United States v. Alkhabaz (Baker)*, 104 F.3d 1492, 1495 (6th Cir. 1997)("to constitute a communication containing a threat under Section 875(c), a communication must be such that a reasonable person (1) would take the statement as a serious express of an intention to inflict bodily harm (the mens rea), and (2) would perceive such expression as being communicated to effect some change or achieve some goal through intimidation (the actus reus)"); *United States v. Stewart*, 411 F.3d 825, 828 (7th Cir. 2005)("guilt is not dependent upon what the defendant intended, but whether the recipient could reasonably have regarded the defendant's statement as a threat")(court declines to follow contradictory Ninth Circuit precedent, id. at 828 n4).

[223] *United States v. Hinkson,* 349 F.Supp.2d 1350, 1355 (D. Idaho 2004) ("Certain expressions, including 'vehement, caustic, and sometimes unpleasantly sharp attacks on Government and public officials[,]' may be protected free speech")(citing *Watts v. United States*, 394 U.S. 705, 708 (1969)); *United States v. Bly*, 510 F.3d 453, 458 (4th Cir. 2007). Moreover, "generally, a person who informs someone that he or she is in danger from a third party has not made a threat," *New York ex rel. Spitzer v. Operation Rescue National*, 273 F.3d 184, 196 (2d Cir. 2001).

[224] *United States v. Patrick*, 117 F.3d 375, 377 (8th Cir. 1997)("that Patrick's threat was contingent upon his release from prison does not save him from violating section 876"); *United States v. Viefhaus*, 168 F.3d 392, 396 (10th Cir. 1999); *United States v. Bly*, 510 F.3d 453, 459 (4th Cir. 2007); as the phrase "your money or your life" demonstrates, contingent threats are an essential component of robbery and extortion.

[225] *United States v. Cassel*, 408 F.3d 622, 627-28 (9th Cir. 2005); *United States v. Saunders*, 166 F.3d 907, 914 (7th Cir. 1999); *United States v. Martin*, 163 F.3d 1212, 1216 (10th Cir. 1998).

[226] *United States v. Floyd*, 458 F.3d 844, 849 (8th Cir. 2006); *United States v. Hinkson*, 349 F. Supp. 2d 1350, 1355 (D. Idaho 2004).

[227] *United States v. Fulmer*, 108 F.3d 1486, 1492 (1st Cir. 1997); *United States v. Malik*, 16 F.3d 45, 49 (2nd Cir. 1994).

[228] *United States v. England*, 507 F.3d 581, 589 (7th Cir. 2007); *United States v. Francis*, 164 F.3d 120, 123 (2d Cir. 1999); *United States v. Morales*, 272 F.3d 284, 287 (5th Cir. 2001). *United States v. Stewart*, 411 F.3d 825, 828 (7th Cir. 2005) ("the government must prove that the statement came in a context or under such circumstances wherein a reasonable person would foresee that the statement would be interpreted by those to whom the maker communicates a statement as a serious expression of an intention to inflict bodily harm upon or to take the life of [another individual].")

[229] *United States v. Korab*, 893 F.2d 212, 214-15 (9th Cir. 1989).

[230] *United States v. Darby*, 37 F.3d at 1063-64; see also, *United States v. Kammersell*, 196 F.3d 1137, 1139-140 (10th Cir. 1999)(a threatening computer message from defendant in Utah to his girlfriend's place of employment within the same state constituted transmission of a threatening communication in interstate commerce because the message was transmitted by way of the defendant's service provider's main server in Virginia; see also *United States v. Guerva*, 408 F.3d 252, 259 (5th Cir. 2005)(court finding that threat that led to the temporary closing of a federal building and the shutting down of various federal agencies resulted in threat affecting interstate commerce).

[231] ". . . A civil action for a violation of this section may be brought only if the conduct involves 1 of the factors set forth in clause (i), (ii), (iii), (iv), or (v) of subsection (a)(5)(B) . . ." 18 U.S.C. 1030(g). The qualifying circumstances described in clauses (a)(5)(B)(i) through (v) are: "(i) loss to 1 or more persons during any 1-year period (and, for purposes of an investigation, prosecution, or other proceeding brought by the United States only, loss resulting from a related course of conduct affecting 1 or more other protected computers) aggregating at least $5,000 in value; (ii) the modification or impairment, or potential modification or impairment, of the medical examination, diagnosis, treatment, or care of 1 or more individuals; (iii) physical injury to any person; (iv) a threat to public health or safety; or (v) damage affecting a computer system used by or for a government entity

in furtherance of the administration of justice, national defense, or national security."

[232] For a general discussion see *Elements of Offense Proscribed by the Hobbs Act (18 USCS §1951) Against Racketeering in Interstate or Foreign Commerce*, 4 ALR FED. 881.

[233] *United States v. Davis*, 473 F.3d 680, 681-83 (6th Cir. 2007); *United States v. Mitov*, 460 F.3d 901, 908 (7th Cir. 2006); *United States v. Vega Molina*, 407 F.3d 511, 526 (1st Cir 2005); *United States v. Vallejo*, 297 F.3d 1154, 1166 (11th Cir. 2002); *United States v. Malone*, 222 F.3d 1286, 1294-295 (10th Cir. 2000). Some circuits may be more demanding where the victim is an individual rather than a business, *United States v. Lynch*, 282 F.3d 1049, 1052-55 (9th Cir. 2002) (requiring greater commerce showing the case of individual victims and describing views of other circuits); *United States v. Mann*, 493 F.3d 484, 494-95 (5th Cir. 2007).

[234] *Sanchez v. Triple-S Management, Corp.*, 492 F.3d 1, 12 (1st Cir. 2007); *United States v. Mitov*, 460 F.3d 901, 907 (7th Cir. 2006); *United States v. Cruzado-Laureano*, 404 F.3d 470, 481 (1st Cir. 2005);*United States v. Edwards*, 303 F.3d 606, 635 (5th Cir. 2002); *United States v. Collins*, 78 F.3d 1021, 1029-30 (6th Cir. 1996); *United States v. Middlemiss*, 217 F.3d 112, 118 (2nd Cir. 2000).

[235] Compare *National Organization for Women, Inc. v. Scheidler*, 267 F.3d 687, 709 (7th Cir.2001), rev'd, 537 U.S. 393 (2003)(rejecting a contention that neither women's right to knowingly so deposits as aforesaid, any communication, for the purpose aforesaid receive medical services from abortion clinics nor the clinics' right to provide such services constituted "property" received under threat for Hobbs Act purposes), and *United States v. Gigante*, 39 F.3d 42, 49-51 (2d Cir. 1 994)(holding that the act extended to a benefit realized when the victim of the threat agreed not to engage in competition bidding on a public contract against with firms paying kickbacks to the extortionists); with *Town of West Hartford v. Operation Rescue*, 915 F.2d 92, 101-2 (2nd Cir. 1 990)(despite recognition that "'property' under the [Hobbs] Act 'includes in a broad sense, any valuable right considered as a source or element of wealth' including a right to solicit business . . . the term 'property' cannot plausible be construed to encompass altered official conduct," i.e., increased police and other emergency services), and *United States v. Edwards*, 303 F.3d 606, 635 (5th Cir. 2002)(noting that the "property" threatened for Hobbs Act purposes does not include potential benefits or opportunities). The Supreme Court subsequently resolved the Hobbs Act issue – not by determining whether

the extraction of intangible property is sufficient to constitute extortion under the act – but by concluding that the Hobbs extortion requires that the offender "obtain" something, merely compelling the victim to forego the exercise of a prerogative is insufficient, *Scheidler v. National Organization for Women, Inc.*, 537 U.S. 393, 402-10 (2003). For a discussion on the Hobbs Act in relation to social protest activity and the meaning of property in that context, see Kristal S. Stippich, *Behind the Words: Interpreting the Hobbs Act Requirement of "Obtaining of Property From Another,*" 36 JOHN MARSHALL LAW REVIEW 295 (2003).

Congress' uncertainty notwithstanding, at least one district court has confirmed the extraterritorial application of the Hobbs Act, 18 U.S.C. 371 (conspiracy), 18 U.S.C. 1029 (access device offenses), as well as paragraphs 1030(a)(7)(extortion) and 1030(a)(4)(fraud) to misconduct arising out of an overseas extortionate threat against a commercial computer system in this country, United States v. Ivanov, 175 F.Supp.2d 367 (D.Conn. 2001).

[236] "Whoever, with intent to extort from any person, firm, association, or corporation, any money or other thing of value, transmits in interstate or foreign commerce any communication containing any threat to injure the property . . . of the addressee or of another. . . shall be fined under this title or imprisoned not more than two years, or both," 18 U.S.C. 875(d).

[237] "Whoever, with intent to extort from any person any money or other thing of value, knowingly so deposits or causes to be delivered, as aforesaid, any communication, with or without a name or designating mark subscribed thereto, addressed to any other person and containing any threat to injure the property . . . of the addressee or of another . . . . shall be fined under this title or imprisoned not more than two years, or both. If such a communication is addressed to a United Stats judge, a federal law enforcement officer, or an official who is covered by section 1114 [any federal employee], the individual shall be fined under this title, imprisoned not more than 10 years, or both," 18 U.S.C. 876(d).

[238] ". . . Whoever, with intent to extort from any person any money or other thing of value fined under this title or imprisoned not more than two years, or both," 18 U.S.C. 877.

[239] "A person who receives, possesses, conceals, or disposes of any money or other property which was obtained from the commission of any offense under this chapter that is punishable by imprisonment for more than 1 year, knowing the same to have been unlawfully obtained, shall be imprisoned not more than 3 years, fined under this title, or both," 18 U.S.C. 880.

[240] See *United States v. Maneri,* 353 F.3d 165, 168 (2d Cir. 2003)(thing of value included opportunity for sexual encounter); U*nited States v. Freeman*, 208 F .3d 332, 341 (1st Cir. 2000)(night club owner's special treatment of police officer including access to dancers' dressing room constituted a thing of value); *United States v. Marmolejo*, 89 F.3d 1185, 1192-193 (5th Cir. 1996)(citing a wide range of intangible property benefits found to constitute "things of value" under various federal criminal statutes); *United States v. Bryant*, 117 F.3d 1464, 1468 n.7 (D.C.Cir. 1997)(noting that a forbearance from arrest constitutes a "thing of value" for purposes of 18 U.S.C. 912 even in a case where two members of the three judge panel expressed the view that the defendant should never have been charged, prosecuted or convicted); *United States v. Collins*, 56 F.3d 1416, 1420 (D.C.Cir. 1995)(noting the widespread acceptance of an expansive reading of the term "thing of value" the purposes of the theft of federal property statute, 18 U.S.C. 641). The things of value are not limited to those things that can be lawfully possessed, see e.g., *United States v. Sargent*, 504 F.3d 767, 770-71 (9th Cir. 2007)(marijuana); *United States v. Fink*, 502 F.3d 585, 586 (6th Cir. 2007)(child pornography).

[241] *United States v. Salvatore*, 110 F.3d 1131, 1139-141 (5th Cir. 1 997)(noting the *McNally- Carpenter* distinction and the split of appellate courts on the question of whether unissued licenses may constitute "property" interests for purposes of the mail fraud statute, 18 U.S.C. 1341, a conflict which the Supreme Court subsequently resolved in *Cleveland v. United States*, 531 U.S. 12, 26-7 (2000) when it concluded that a state had not been defrauded of "property" for the purposes of section 1341 when it was fraudulently induced by issue a license); *United States v. Delano*, 55 F.3d 720, 726-27 (2d Cir. 1995)(holding that labor or services cannot be considered "property" for purposes of a RICO charged based on an extortionate predicate offense). *United States v. Hedaithy*, 392 F.3d 580, 584 (3d Cir. 2004) (court found that mail fraud violation occurred when would-be test takers had others take a standardized test in their place; the court found that the testing service's property interests were violated because of the unauthorized use of its copyrighted and confidential materials and because, in obtaining a score report, the defendants possessed the "embodiment of the services that ETS provides").

[242] "Whoever . . . knowingly and with intent to defraud traffics in or uses one or more unauthorized access devices during any one-year period, and by such conduct obtains anything of value aggregating $1,000 or more during that period . . . shall, if the offense affects interstate or foreign commerce, be

punished as provided in subsection (c) of this section," 18 U.S.C. 1029(a)(2). Violations are punishable by imprisonment for not more than 10 years and/or a fine of not more than $250,000, 18 U.S.C. 1029(c)(1)

[243] Prosecution under paragraph 1029(a)(2) requires a loss of at least $1,000 over the course of a year and that the device permit access to an "account," 18 U.S.C. 1029(e)(1)(defining "access device"); paragraph 1030(a)(6) imposes neither burden upon a prosecution. This is probably why paragraph 1030(a)(6) is punishable as a misdemeanor while paragraph 1029(a)(2) is a 10 year felony.

[244] To establish wire fraud, the government must show an interstate wire transmission in furtherance of a scheme to defraud another of money or property, *United States v. Mann*, 493 U.S. 484, 493 (5th Cir. 2007); *United States v. Allen*, 491 F.3d 178, 185 (4th Cir. 2007); *United States v. Dowlin*, 408 F.3d 647, 658 n.5 (10th Cir. 2005); *United States v. Owens*, 301 F.3d 521, 528 (7th Cir. 2002).

[245] For a discussion of federal espionage laws generally see, 70 AMERICAN JURISPRUDENCE, 2D EDITION, *Sedition, Subversive Activities, and Treason* §§17-44; see also, Bazan, *Espionage and the Death Penalty*, 41 FEDERAL BAR NEWS & JOURNAL 615 (1994); Vladeck, *Inchoate Liability and the Espionage Act: The Statutory Framework and the Freedom of the Press*, 1 HARVARD LAW &J POLICY REVIEW 219 (2007).

[246] 18 U.S.C. 1030 (1982 ed. & 1984 Supp.); H.Rept.98-894 at 21 (1984). Compare the language of 1030(a)(1) with that of 18 U.S.C. 793(e)("Whoever having unauthorized possession of, access to, or control over any document, writing, code book, signal book, sketch, photograph, photographic negative, blueprint, plan, map, model, instrument, appliance, or note relating to the national defense, or information relating to the national defense which information the possessor has reason to believe could be used to the injury of the United States or to the advantage of any foreign nation, willfully communicates, delivers, transmits or causes to be communicated, delivered, or transmitted, or attempts to communicate, deliver, transmit or cause to be communicated, delivered, or transmitted the same to any person not entitled to receive it, or willfully retains the same and fails to deliver it to the officer or employee of the United States entitled to receive it").

[247] "Although there is considerable overlap between 18 U.S.C. 793(3) and section 1030(a)(1), as amended by the NII Protection Act, the two statutes would not reach exactly the same conduct. Section 1030(a)(1) wold target those persons who deliberately break into a computer to obtain properly

classified Government secrets then try to peddle those secrets to others, including foreign governments. In other words, unlike existing espionage laws prohibiting the theft and peddling of Government secrets to foreign agents, section 1030(a)(1) would require proof that the individual knowingly used a computer without authority, or in excess of authority, for the purpose of obtaining classified information. In this sense then, it is the use of the computer which is being proscribed, not the unauthorized possession of, access to, or control over the classified information itself," S.Rept. 104-357 at 6-7.

[248] H.Rept. 98-894 at 21 (1984)("As the Supreme Court stated in Gorin v. U.S., (312 U.S. 19, 28), 'This requires those prosecuted to have acted in bad faith. The sanctions apply only when scienter is established'").

[249] See generally, CRS Report 97-805, *Espionage in the United States: Individuals Arrested 1993-1998*, by Suzanne Cavanagh and Stephanie Flagg; and CRS Report 93-531, *Individuals Arrested on Charges of Espionage Against the United States Government*, by Suzanne Cavanagh.

[250] Olivenbaum, *<CTRL><ALT><DELETE>: Rethinking Federal Computer Crime Legislation*, 27 SETON HALL LAW REVIEW 574, 594-95 (1997), citing *United States v. Poulsen*, 41 F.3d 1330 (9th Cir. 1994).

[251] "Whoever, for the purpose of obtaining information respecting the national defense with intent or reason to believe that the information is to be used to the injury of the United States, or to the advantage of any foreign nation, goes upon, enters, flies over, or otherwise obtains information concerning any vessel, aircraft, work of defense, navy yard, naval station, submarine base, fueling station, fort, battery, torpedo station, dockyard, canal, railroad, arsenal, camp, factory, mine, telegraph, telephone, wireless, or signal station, building, office, research laboratory or station or other place connected with the national defense owned or constructed, or in progress of construction by the United States or under the control of the United States, or of any of its officers, departments, or agencies, or within the exclusive jurisdiction of the United States, or any place in which any vessel, aircraft, arms, munitions, or other materials or instruments for use in time of war are being made, prepared, repaired, stored, or are the subject of research or development, under any contract or agreement with the United States, or any department or agency thereof, or with any person on behalf of the United States, or otherwise on behalf of the United States, or any prohibited place so designated by the President by proclamation in time of war or in case of national emergency in which anything for the use of the Army, Navy, or Air Force is being prepared or constructed or stored, information

as to which prohibited place the President has determined would be prejudicial to the national defense . . . Shall be fined under this title or imprisoned not more than ten years, or both," 18 U.S.C. 793(a).

[252] "Whoever, for the purpose aforesaid, and with like intent or reason to believe, copies, takes, makes, or obtains, or attempts to copy, take, make, or obtain, any sketch, photograph, photographic negative, blueprint, plan, map, model, instrument, appliance, document, writing, or note of anything connected with the national defense . . . Shall be fined under this title or imprisoned not more than ten years, or both,"18 U.S.C. 793(b).

[253] "Whoever, for the purpose aforesaid, receives or obtains or agrees or attempts to receive or obtain from any person, or from any source whatever, any document, writing, code book, signal book, sketch, photograph, photographic negative, blueprint, plan, map, model, instrument, appliance, or note, of anything connected with the national defense, knowing or having reason to believe, at the time he receives or obtains, or agrees or attempts to receive or obtain it, that it has been or will be obtained, taken, made, or disposed of by any person contrary to the provisions of this chapter . . . Shall be fined under this title or imprisoned not more than ten years, or both,"1 8 U.S.C. 793(c).

[254] "Whoever, lawfully having possession of, access to, control over, or being entrusted with any document, writing, code book, signal book, sketch, photograph, photographic negative, blueprint, plan, map, model, instrument, appliance, or note relating to the national defense, or information relating to the national defense which information the possessor has reason to believe could be used to the injury of the United States or to the advantage of any foreign nation, willfully communicates, delivers, transmits or causes to be communicated, delivered, or transmitted or attempts to communicate, deliver, transmit or cause to be communicated, delivered or transmitted the same to any person not entitled to receive it, or willfully retains the same and fails to deliver it on demand to the officer or employee of the United States entitled to receive it . . . Shall be fined under this title or imprisoned not more than ten years, or both,"18 U.S.C. 793(d).

[255] Whoever having unauthorized possession of, access to, or control over any document, writing, code book, signal book, sketch, photograph, photographic negative, blueprint, plan, map, model, instrument, appliance, or note relating to the national defense, or information relating to the national defense which information the possessor has reason to believe could be used to the injury of the United States or to the advantage of any foreign nation, willfully communicates, delivers, transmits or causes to be

communicated, delivered, or transmitted, or attempts to communicate, deliver, transmit or cause to be communicated, delivered, or transmitted the same to any person not entitled to receive it, or willfully retains the same and fails to deliver it to the officer or employee of the United States entitled to receive it . . . Shall be fined under this title or imprisoned not more than ten years, or both," 18 U.S.C. 793(e)

[256] "Whoever, being entrusted with or having lawful possession or control of any document, writing, code book, signal book, sketch, photograph, photographic negative, blueprint, plan, map, model, instrument, appliance, note, or information, relating to the national defense, (1) through gross negligence permits the same to be removed from its proper place of custody or delivered to anyone in violation of his trust, or to be lost, stolen, abstracted, or destroyed, or (2) having knowledge that the same has been illegally removed from its proper place of custody or delivered to anyone in violation of his trust, or lost, or stolen, abstracted, or destroyed, and fails to make prompt report of such loss, theft, abstraction, or destruction to his superior officer . . . Shall be fined under this title or imprisoned not more than ten years, or both," 18 U.S.C. 793(f).

[257] "Whoever, with intent or reason to believe that it is to be used to the injury of the United States or to the advantage of a foreign nation, communicates, delivers, or transmits, or attempts to communicate, deliver, or transmit, to any foreign government, or to any faction or party or military or naval force within a foreign country, whether recognized or unrecognized by the United States, or to any representative, officer, agent, employee, subject, or citizen thereof, either directly or indirectly, any document, writing, code book, signal book, sketch, photograph, photographic negative, blueprint, plan, map, model, note, instrument, appliance, or information relating to the national defense, shall be punished by death or by imprisonment for any term of years or for life, except that the sentence of death shall not be imposed unless the jury or, if there is no jury, the court, further finds that the offense resulted in the identification by a foreign power (as defined in section 101(a) of the Foreign Intelligence Surveillance Act of 1978) of an individual acting as an agent of the United States and consequently in the death of that individual, or directly concerned nuclear weaponry, military spacecraft or satellites, early warning systems, or other means of defense or retaliation against large-scale attack; war plans; communications intelligence or cryptographic information; or any other major weapons system or major element of defense strategy," 18 U.S.C. 794(a).

[258] "Whoever, in time of war, with intent that the same shall be communicated to the enemy, collects, records, publishes, or communicates, or attempts to elicit any information with respect to the movement, numbers, description, condition, or disposition of any of the Armed Forces, ships, aircraft, or war materials of the United States, or with respect to the plans or conduct, or supposed plans or conduct of any naval or military operations, or with respect to any works or measures undertaken for or connected with, or intended for the fortification or defense of any place, or any other information relating to the public defense, which might be useful to the enemy, shall be punished by death or by imprisonment for any term of years or for life," 18 U.S.C. 794(b).

[259] "(a) Whoever knowingly and willfully communicates, furnishes, transmits, or otherwise makes available to an unauthorized person, or publishes, or uses in any manner prejudicial to the safety or interest of the United States or for the benefit of any foreign government to the detriment of the United States any classified information – (1) concerning the nature, preparation, or use of any code, cipher, or cryptographic system of the United States or any foreign government; or (2) concerning the design, construction, use, maintenance, or repair of any device, apparatus, or appliance used or prepared or planned for use by the United States or any foreign government for cryptographic or communication intelligence purposes; or (3) concerning the communication intelligence activities of the United States or any foreign government; or (4) obtained by the processes of communication intelligence from the communications of any foreign government, knowing the same to have been obtained by such processes – Shall be fined under this title or imprisoned not more than ten years, or both.

As used in subsection (a) of this section – The term 'classified information' means information which, at the time of a violation of this section, is, for reasons of national security, specifically designated by a United States Government Agency for limited or restricted dissemination or distribution; The terms 'code,' 'cipher,' and 'cryptographic system' include in their meanings, in addition to their usual meanings, any method of secret writing and any mechanical or electrical device or method used for the purpose of disguising or concealing the contents, significance, or meanings of communications; The term `foreign government' includes in its meaning any person or persons acting or purporting to act for or on behalf of any faction, party, department, agency, bureau, or military force of or within a foreign country, or for or on behalf of any government or any person or persons purporting to act as a government within a foreign country, whether or not such government is recognized by the United States; The term 'communication intelligence' means all procedures and methods used in the interception of communications and the obtaining of information from such communications by other than the intended recipients; The term 'unauthorized person' means any person who, or agency which, is not authorized to receive information of the categories set forth in subsection (a) of this section, by the President, or by the head of a department or agency of the United States Government which is expressly designated by the President to engage in communication intelligence activities for the United States.

Nothing in this section shall prohibit the furnishing, upon lawful demand, of information to any regularly constituted committee of the Senate or House of Representatives of the United States of America, or joint committee thereof."

[260] "Whoever, intending or knowing that the offense will benefit any foreign government, foreign instrumentality, or foreign agent, knowingly – (1) steals, or without authorization appropriates, takes, carries away, or conceals, or by fraud, artifice, or deception obtains a trade secret; (2) without authorization copies, duplicates, sketches, draws, photographs, downloads, uploads, alters, destroys, photocopies, replicates, transmits, delivers, sends, mails, communicates, or conveys a trade secret; (3) receives, buys, or possesses a trade secret, knowing the same to have been stolen or appropriated, obtained, or converted without authorization; (4) attempts to commit any offense described in any of paragraphs (1) through (3); or (5) conspires with one or more other persons to commit any offense described in any of paragraphs (1) through (3), and one or more of such persons do any act to effect the object of the conspiracy, – shall, except as provided in subsection (b), be fined not more than $500,000 or imprisoned not more than 15 years, or both," 18 U.S.C. 1 831(a).

INDEX

B

C

D

S

W